HOW TO SURVIVE IN
ANCIENT
EGYPT

For Brian

HOW TO SURVIVE IN
ANCIENT
EGYPT

CHARLOTTE BOOTH

PEN & SWORD **HISTORY**

AN IMPRINT OF PEN & SWORD BOOKS LTD
YORKSHIRE - PHILADELPHIA

First published in Great Britain in 2020 by
PEN AND SWORD HISTORY
An imprint of
Pen & Sword Books Ltd
Yorkshire – Philadelphia

ISBN 978 1 52675 349 6

Typeset in Times New Roman 11.5/14 by
Aura Technology and Software Services, India.
Printed and bound in the UK by TJ International Ltd.

Pen & Sword Books Limited incorporates the imprints of Atlas, Archaeology,
Aviation, Discovery, Family History, Fiction, History, Maritime, Military, Military
Classics, Politics, Select, Transport, True Crime, Air World, Frontline Publishing,
Leo Cooper, Remember When, Seaforth Publishing, The Praetorian Press,
Wharncliffe Local History, Wharncliffe Transport, Wharncliffe True Crime and
White Owl.

For a complete list of Pen & Sword titles please contact
PEN & SWORD BOOKS LIMITED
47 Church Street, Barnsley, South Yorkshire, S70 2AS, England
E-mail: enquiries@pen-and-sword.co.uk
Website: www.pen-and-sword.co.uk

Or
PEN AND SWORD BOOKS
1950 Lawrence Rd, Havertown, PA 19083, USA
E-mail: Uspen-and-sword@casematepublishers.com
Website: www.penandswordbooks.com

Contents

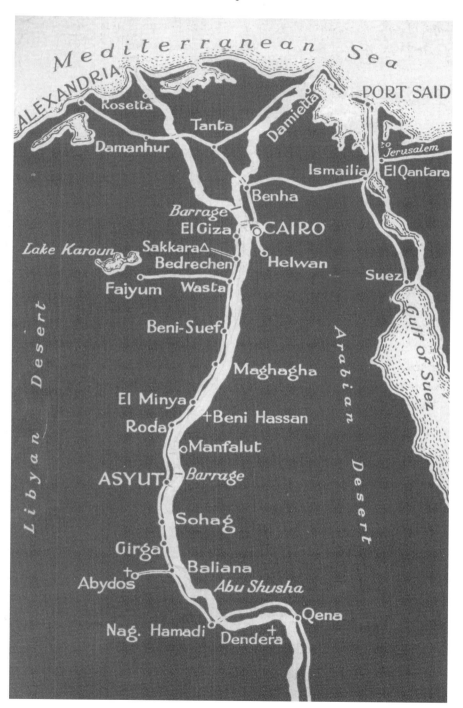

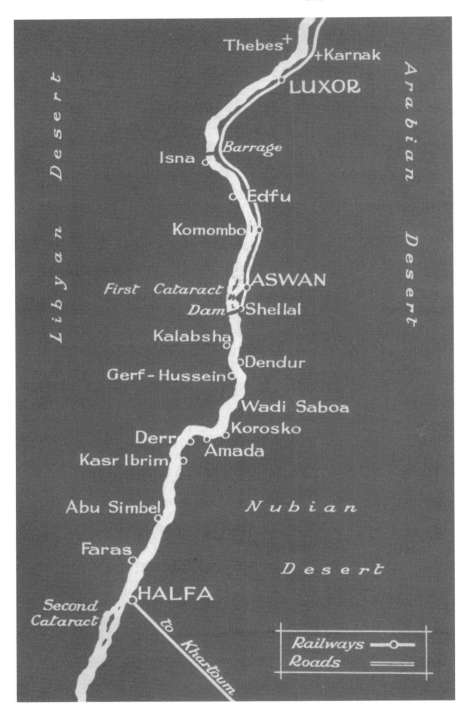

Illustrations

All photographs are provided courtesy of BKB Photography unless otherwise stated.

All illustrations are drawn by the author.

Maps–Courtesy of the Thomas Cook Archive.

1 Amenhotep III, Luxor Museum. (Photograph by the author).
2 *sm3 t3wy* symbol on the base of a statue of Ramses II at Abu Simbel.
3 Sphinx, Giza. (Photograph by the author).
4 *hk3 h3swt* (Hyksos) traders from the Middle Kingdom tomb of Khnumnhotep III at Beni Hasan. (Picture courtesy of Ulla Kaer Andersen).
5 Hatshepsut and Senenmut graffiti, found in the Deir el Bahri cliffs.
6 Four-roomed house (drawing adapted from Uphill, 2001, Fig 10).
7 Amun-Min and his sacred lettuce, Karnak.
8 A laundry list from Deir el Medina (drawing after McDowell 1999, p.61).
9 Amenhotep, Son of Hapu the scribe of Amenhotep III, Luxor Museum.
10 Hathor nursing the king, Edfu.
11 Professional mourners, tomb of Khaemhat, Valley of the Nobles, Thebes.
12 Seven Hathors, temple of Ramses III at Medinet Habu.
13 Bes, Denderah.
14 Procession of dancers, Red Chapel of Hatshepsut, Karnak. (Photograph by the author).
15 Funerary banquet, tomb of Paheri, El Kab.
16 Shower, palace at Medinet Habu. (Photograph by the author).
17 Perfume making, tomb of Iymery, Giza.
18 Perfume cone worn by Tiy, the wife of Ay, at Amarna.

Timeline

Pre-dynastic Period
Before 3050 BCE

Early Dynastic Period
Dynasty O: 3150-3050 BCE
Dynasty 1: 3050-2890 BCE
Dynasty 2: 2890-2686 BCE

Old Kingdom
Dynasty 3: 2686-2613 BCE
Dynasty 4: 2613-2500 BCE
Dynasty 5: 2498-2345 BCE
Dynasty 6: 2345-2333 BCE

First Intermediate Period
Dynasty 7 and 8: 2180-2160 BCE
Dynasty 9 and 10: 2160-2040 BCE

Middle Kingdom
Dynasty 11: 2134-1991 BCE
Dynasty 12: 1991-1782 BCE

Second Intermediate Period
Dynasty 13: 1782-1650 BCE
Dynasty 14: ?
Dynasty 15: 1663-1555 BCE
Dynasty 16: 1663-1555 BCE
Dynasty 17: 1663-1570 BCE

New Kingdom
Dynasty 18: 1570-1293 BCE
Dynasty 19: 1308-1185 BCE
Dynasty 20: 1185-1070 BCE

Third Intermediate period
High Priests (Thebes): 1080-945 BCE
Dynasty 21 (Tanis): 1069-945 BCE
Dynasty 22 (Tanis): 945-715 BCE
Dynasty 23 (Leontopolis): 818-715 BCE
Dynasty 24 (Sais): 727-715 BCE
Dynasty 25(Nubians): 747-656 BCE
Dynasty 26 (Sais): 664-525 BCE

Late Period
Dynasty 27 (Persian): 525-404 BCE
Dynasty 28: 404-399 BCE
Dynasty 29: 399-380 BCE
Dynasty 30: 380-343 BCE
Dynasty 31: 343-332 BCE

Graeco-Roman Period
Macedonian Kings: 332-305 BCE
Ptolemaic Period: 305-30 BCE

Introduction

The book that you are holding in your hands is a history book, but not an ordinary one. You as the reader are an important part of the story, and with a little bit of imagination you can bring this book and the world it describes to life.

This book will transport you to ancient Thebes – modern Luxor – in the year 1360 BCE during the glory years of Amenhotep III, in what is now known as the eighteenth dynasty. Amenhotep III ruled between 1386 BCE and 1349 BCE and was the father of one of the most famous and

Amenhotep III, Luxor Museum. (Photograph by the author).

controversial kings in ancient Egyptian history, Akhenaten. Of course at the time, no one knew the controversy Akhenaten would bring.

As the reader, you are to imagine you are an 'outsider' to Thebes; an expat if you will. You are a male who has recently moved to the religious capital of Egypt and needs a handy guide to learn the ropes in your newly adopted city. This is essentially the expat guide to ancient Thebes, advising on shopping, entertaining, finding work, how to avoid the magistrates and what to do if you are taken ill. Whilst in modern times it is not unusual for unaccompanied women to move abroad, in ancient Egypt this would have been very unusual. Therefore I am making the assumption that the expat reading this guide is male, as a reflection of their times rather than ours. Women will, of course, be addressed and business opportunities open to them will be discussed.

When writing a book of this kind, there are some things that need to be taken into consideration. As it is aimed at a reader in 1360 BCE, elements of Egyptian history will be described in the present tense rather than the past tense. References to 'you' are addressing the expat visitor to Thebes and offer helpful advice on various aspects of life.

As this is a history book with a difference, information will also be included that someone living in Thebes during the eighteenth dynasty would not know, but modern Egyptologists do. These have been included as text boxes and snippets of information entitled 'Did you know?' These will provide you with information not readily available for the ancient Egyptians.

Conversely, there are, of course, many things that an expat living in Thebes during this time would know instinctively and would not need to be explained in a guide and therefore these will be explained here for the benefit of the modern reader.

Things You Should Know

The Nile

Egypt (or Kemet as it was known) was a riverine society which relied heavily on the Nile for agriculture, food and transportation. The river was therefore a fundamental aspect of their lives, forming the basis of religion, work, food production and the calendar.

The Nile flowed from the south to the north through a fertile area in the north of Egypt – or Lower Egypt – characterised by numerous branches, known as the Delta, and out into the Mediterranean Sea.

The south of Egypt, or Upper Egypt, is where ancient Thebes stood and is often referred to as the Nile valley. The fertile Nile valley covered an area of approximately one mile on each side of the river. This was the extent of the land that could be irrigated adequately. The amount of habitable land did not vary much over the millennia; the Nile valley and the Delta combined formed only 34,000sq km of land. With modern irrigation techniques and less reliance on the Nile inundation, this fertile area of land has increased, although not by much; in 2016 the amount of arable land in Egypt was 38,202sq km.

During stable periods of Egyptian history, such as during the reign of Amenhotep III, the king ruled both Upper and Lower Egypt, bearing the title of the dual king. During less stable periods a king might only rule the north or the south. Ruling a divided Egypt meant the king was not considered a true king.

Boundaries

This limited inhabitable land was essentially the key to the success of Egypt as it acted as their main defence. Both to the east and west of the irrigated land was a wide expanse of desert, which acted as a natural boundary and meant the residents of the Nile Valley were isolated from their neighbours.

The army traversed the desert to participate in expeditions to trade, mine or extend the borders, but this was considered a very dangerous journey to embark on, due not only to the inhospitable environment but also the risk of attack by desert tribes. Egypt, however, was able to defend itself against potential attacks from the desert and was not invaded until later periods of Egyptian history.

Generally, non-Egyptians who travelled to Egypt were welcomed and absorbed into the indigenous society. For example, many people in the Middle Kingdom believed that the Hyksos – or Rulers of Foreign Lands – invaded Egypt and took over the throne (see below). However, archaeological evidence from their capital city of Tell el Dab'a (Avaris) in the Delta indicates the Asiatic community had, in fact, been living at the site for at least a century before they took control; first of the city, then the surrounding towns and finally both north and south of Egypt.

The northern boundary of Egypt was the western coastline of the Mediterranean Sea as well as a string of fortresses along the eastern border of the Delta. The Middle Kingdom prophecies of Neferti (which only survive in eighteenth dynasty resources) refer to this string of fortresses as the Wall of the Ruler: 'One will build the Walls-of-the-Ruler, to bar Asiatics from entering Egypt. They shall beg water as supplicants, so as to let their cattle drink. Then order will return to its seat while chaos is driven away.'

This Middle Kingdom chain of fortresses was abandoned during the Second Intermediate Period when Egypt was divided with the Hyksos rulers in the north and the Theban rulers in the south. However, Sety I (1291-1278 BCE) reinstated a military presence in this area. There is archaeological evidence of fortresses along the Ways of Horus, along the desert route out of the Nile Delta through the Sinai towards Palestine. None of these fortresses are extant archaeologically today. However, Ramses III built the temple of Medinet Habu at Thebes with an adjoining palace in the style of a military fortress and provides some insight into what a late New Kingdom fortress looked like.

The southern boundary of Egypt naturally lay at the site of the first cataract in Nubia, just south of modern Aswan. The cataracts were a series of rocky outcrops in the river forming a natural defence, which was difficult to cross and easy for the Egyptians to defend.

This region remained the southern boundary of Egypt throughout the dynastic period, although during prosperous reigns, when there was a strong army, the boundary was pushed further south. For example, during the reign of Amenhotep III the boundary was pushed as far south as Semna, 15 miles south of the second cataract. Semna currently sits under Lake Nasser, an artificial lake created when the Aswan High Dam was constructed in the 1960s.

There was also a series of fortresses along the southern boundary which included Semna, Mirgissa, Uronati and Buhen. They were abandoned in the twentieth dynasty. These fortresses were all destroyed when the Aswan High Dam was built in the 1960s and also remain under the depths of Lake Nasser. Luckily, research was carried out by Walter Bryan Emery (1903-1971) in the late 1950s at Buhen, prior to their destruction, which is invaluable when studying the Egyptian military or foreign policy.

Lake Nasser is the largest man-made lake in the world, with eighty-three per cent of it in Egypt. It is 479km (298 miles) long and 16km (9.9 miles) across.

Nomes

Within the boundaries of Egypt the land was further divided into administrative regions known as *nomes*. There were twenty-two *nomes* in Upper Egypt and twenty in Lower Egypt. Each *nome* had its own chieftain, laws, gods, standards, practices and taboos. Although each *nome* was governed locally, ultimately they were all under the centralised control of the king, although the king, or the vizier on his behalf, only got involved in very serious circumstances.

Ancient Thebes was in the fourth *nome* of Upper Egypt, known to the ancient Egyptians as Waset. Waset was a provincial town until the Middle Kingdom when it became the administrative capital and remained so throughout the New Kingdom. The city was also the central seat of the god Amun. During the New Kingdom the power of Amun increased until, during the tumultuous Third Intermediate Period, the High Priests of Amun actually took over the throne of Egypt.

Nile Inundation

There was very little rainfall in ancient Egypt and even today in the Delta region there is only approximately 100-200mm of rain per year. The people relied solely on the river Nile and the annual inundation for their water supply. The Nile flooded between July and October, putting most of the land on either side of the river under water. This washed all the salt out of the soil and, as the water receded, a rich, fertile silt was deposited over the land. It was this fertile silt that gave Egypt the name of Kemet, or 'Black Land'.

The main crops were then sown in October or November, ready for harvesting in April. However, should the inundation be too low, then the fields would not be irrigated enough and there would be famine. Conversely, should the inundation be too high then it would take longer for the water to recede, which affected the planting season and could result in the failure of crops and, consequently, famine.

The Egyptians were a very practical people and used Nilometers placed at major temples throughout Upper Egypt – including Philae, Edfu, Esna, Kom Ombo and Denderah – to measure the movement of the river. These were in the form of staircases or corridors, which extended down into the river. These measured the water levels at different times of the year, and by comparing data from previous years the priests could predict the level of the inundation and therefore make preparations in order to prevent a famine should the inundation predictions be unfavourable. Although records were kept from the Early Dynastic Period, all the Nilometers that have survived are from the Late Period or later.

Festivals were held alongside the Nilometers to celebrate the appearance of the annual inundation. There are long-standing local rumours that to celebrate the rising of the Nile, a young virgin was thrown into the rising river to appease the gods and encourage them to provide a good flood.

The regular threat of famine is an important aspect of ancient Egyptian life. Wages were paid in food rations, and there was no concept of dieting. When you had food you ate, and when you didn't you starved. Therefore, if people had rolls of fat it was a sign of wealth, and something many people aspired to. The majority of people ate a vegetarian diet; not out of choice but out of necessity.

Only the rich could afford to eat meat; the majority of the population survived on vegetables and fish.

The landscape of Thebes was not very different during the time of Amenhotep III than Luxor is today; although, of course, today there are cars, motorised boats and other evidence of industry. However, many ancient crafts and skills are carried on in modern Luxor and it is possible to witness elements of the ancient past, such as traditional fishing and irrigation techniques, and manufacture of bricks out of Nile mud dried in the sun.

Irrigation was essential for ensuring enough food could grow with the limited resources available. Irrigation ditches were cut around the fields and water was lifted from the Nile using a *shaduf*. This device was introduced in the New Kingdom, so at the time this book is set this was considered brand-new technology. The technology is simple but effective and comprised a long pole with a jar on one end and a weight on the other. Once the jar was filled with water, the pole pivoted, lifting the water up to a height of 3m and diverted it into the irrigation channels.

The main difference with the landscape in Egypt is that today the Nile no longer floods annually, and has not done so since the first set of sluices and the dam were built in Aswan in 1830. These were constructed as a means of regulating the water supply and ensuring crops could be grown all year round.

However, the crops for which Egypt is currently famous – sugar and cotton – were unfamiliar to the ancient Egyptians as they were not introduced until the nineteenth century. Ancient Egyptian clothes, therefore, were not made of cotton but linen, which was produced from the cellulose fibres of the flax plant. There were different qualities of linen and we will learn more about this in the section 'Stepping out in Style', on page 101.

Time-keeping

Another element of life in ancient Egypt that was very different to the modern world was telling the time. People told the time by the position of the sun during the day and the stars during the night; a skill most people in the modern world have lost. The Egyptians also had primitive clocks.

Outflow water-clocks were introduced in the Middle Kingdom, possibly during the reign of Amenemhat I (1991-1962 BCE). These clocks comprise a bowl of water with holes marking the twelve hours of day and the twelve hours of the night. As the water drips out, the remaining water marks the current time. It is worth considering, however, that the hours of the day or night were not equal in length, but this was taken into account and the water clocks were generally accurate to within fifteen minutes.

To measure the hours of the night, the temples may also have implemented the use of a *decan* star clock which involved observing the rising and setting of the stars in the night sky. The rising and setting of groups of thirty-six stars, known as *decans*, could be used to identify hours over a period of ten days at a time throughout the year. As each star has a predictable time-line, it can be carefully observed and recorded.

Time was divided into twenty-four hours for each day – no minutes or seconds – thirty days in a month spread over three weeks, and three months in a season. There were three seasons: inundation (*akhet*), June to September; emergence (*peret*), October to February; and harvest (*shemu*), March to May. In total there were 360 days in the year with five additional festival days added to the end of the year to bring it up to 365. These were referred to as 'the five days over the year' and were celebrated as the birthdays of Osiris, Horus, Seth, Isis and Nephthys.

New Year, however, was identified by the heliacal rising of Sopdet, which is more commonly known today as Sirius, rather than a specific date. As a year is approximately 365.25 days long, every four years New Year and the heliacal rising of Sopdet would shift by a day. As the calendar was based on astronomical events rather than counted days New Year did not happen *until* the star rose rather than basing it on dates and number of days.

One would imagine, therefore, that the ancient Egyptians, rather like the modern Egyptians, were a lot more flexible on time than those in the modern west. The only occasions when precision was needed with time-keeping were in the temples and there was a section of the priesthood who were known as hour priests, whose job it was to ensure religious rituals were carried out at the correct hour of the day and night.

Hierarchy

There was a strict social hierarchy in ancient Egypt which has been compared to a pyramid, with the king at the top, a small group of officials beneath him, then the middle classes and, at the bottom, the peasants (essentially, the illiterate masses).

The literacy level was very low, with estimates of less than one per cent of the population being literate. Due to this low level, we have a biased view of ancient Egyptian social history and religion as the archaeological evidence is from the literate middle and upper classes in the form of letters, literary tales, poetry, legal and administrative documents.

This, unfortunately, means the lives of those in the lower part of the hierarchical pyramid, the peasants, are largely invisible, or at best poorly represented. Their lives have to be created using the material culture that remains, which does not include the elaborate houses, tombs or possessions that can be found in the records of the middle and upper classes.

This means that throughout this book, unless specifically stated, the information provided applies only to the middle and upper classes.

Nomenclature

Many of the terms and names of ancient Egyptian things that we are familiar with today would have been unfamiliar to the ancient Egyptians themselves as many of these terms have come to the modern world via the Greek or Arabic languages, or have evolved from the Egyptian terms themselves.

For example, the Egyptians did not call the king pharaoh; that is a Greek interpretation of the term *pr–3a*, which meant 'great house' or 'palace'. The Egyptians referred to the king as *nswt*, which means 'king', or *hm=f*, which means 'His Majesty'.

Even the name of our host city, Thebes, derived from the Greek name, Thebai. The ancient Egyptians knew the city as Waset. Temples like Karnak were also known by different names. Karnak was *ipt swt*, or 'The Most Select of Places', and Deir el Bahri, the temple of Hatshepsut, was known as *Djeser Djeseru*, which meant 'Holy of Holies'.

Royal and god's names have also gone through the same process, so Amenhotep is sometimes referred to by the Greek name Amenophis, and the goddess Isis was known to the Egyptians as Iset. The list of these variants is too long to cover in any detail here, but it is worth being aware that names and words familiar to us were unknown to the people to whom they refer. Throughout this guide the ancient Egyptian terminology will often be used, but the more common name will also be identified for the modern reader.

Another familiar aspect of ancient Egyptian history is the dynastic system. This book will be set in the eighteenth dynasty, but this chronological system was totally unknown to the ancient Egyptians themselves.

The dynastic system was introduced by Manetho in the third century BCE, in an attempt to organise the Egyptian kings. He was an Egyptian priest, but it does need to be considered that he was recording a history that was already two thousand years old; as long as the time between the birth of Jesus and today.

This system concerns what is commonly known today as the pharaonic period and is divided into thirty-one dynasties. Each dynasty was thought to represent one royal family, although this has since been proven to not always be the case. Such a mortal system would not have sat well with the ancient Egyptian belief that the royal blood line could be traced back through history to the time of the gods.

The dynasties were divided into three main periods; the Old Kingdom, the Middle Kingdom and the New Kingdom. These periods were separated by politically unstable eras known as the First, Second and Third Intermediate Periods. The final Intermediate Period was followed by the Late Period, which was characterised by foreign invasions, and the Ptolemaic Period following the invasion of Alexander the Great in 332 BCE. The last queen, Cleopatra VII, was the final ruler before the Romans conquered in 30 BCE. However, this is jumping ahead of the time period which is the focus of this handy guide to living in eighteenth dynasty Thebes

Although this system is flawed it has been adopted by all Egyptologists the world over. However, since this system was introduced, archaeological evidence has been uncovered which pre-dates the first dynasty, meaning a dynasty zero was introduced and then a Pre-Dynastic Period.

So, if the Egyptians did not use dynasties how did they mark the passing of the years? Loosely would be the response. The ancient Egyptians did not have a continuous calendar. Instead, they started counting afresh from the start of every king's reign; so dates were marked as year two of King Ramses for example.

The problem with this system from a modern perspective is that there are no records of when a king died and there are few records that make it clear if there was a co-regency or how long it lasted.

To work out a reign's length archaeologists have to use the latest date known under a particular king. Therefore, the entire chronology can be shifted when a 'new' date is discovered. This is further exacerbated by unpopular reigns, which were ignored, and regnal years of two kings added together. For example, Amenhotep III's son Akhenaten was not popular due to his religious revolution; he eliminated all the gods except the solar deity, the Aten. Therefore, Horemheb, who ruled at the very end of the eighteenth dynasty, adds together the reign length of Akhenaten, Smenkhare, Ay and Tutankhamun to his own, essentially eradicating them from history and totally confusing chronologists who have to decide if he ruled for more than fifty years or thirty-eight years.

This can produce a number of different chronologies with varying dates that correlate with the modern calendar. There are, of course, some dates that we know to be true from other sources. For example, we know that Cleopatra VII died in 30 BCE, and we know that Alexander the Great invaded Egypt in 332 BCE. Anything else before these dates is uncertain, meaning that the modern construct of dynasties makes it much easier to understand.

The dates I have used throughout this guide are from Peter Clayton's *Chronicle of the Pharaohs*. While not necessarily agreeing with all the dates he uses, it is a safe chronology which provides a strong basis upon which to set the book.

The History of Egypt

This book is unusual in the sense that it is set in the middle of a period of history with which we are familiar, and we know what will happen after the date in which this book is set, but the intended expat reader in 1360 BCE would not. The time of 1360 BCE, during the reign of Amenhotep III, would be considered in later years to be a Golden Age; a time that many of the pharaohs looked back on as an ideal. The people living in Egypt at this time did not know they were living in a Golden Age. They had no idea that, in a few years' time, their lives, religion and culture would be overturned by Akhenaten. At this time he was simply a son of the king. They had never heard of Ramses II, and therefore the temples of Karnak and Luxor would have looked very different without the monumental building works he carried out. For example, the awe-inspiring Hypostyle Hall at Karnak did not exist. It would not been constructed until the reign of Ramses I (1293-1291 BCE), approximately seventy years after the date in which this book is set. The end of the pharaonic period, and the invasion of Alexander the Great, was not going to happen for another 1,000 years. This is more or less the same time difference between 2019 and King Aethelred the Unready, when the Vikings were charging across Britain. A lot happened in that time and this has formed the bank of knowledge that we have about the ancient Egyptians.

So, what had happened before 1360 BCE? What would the people of Thebes at this time be familiar with?

Unification of Egypt

As discussed above, Kemet (Egypt) is divided into Upper and Lower Egypt. For a king to be a true king he should rule a unified Kemet. Much of the conflict throughout history is because the country was not unified under a dual king and the politically unstable Intermediate Periods, which fell between the Old, Middle and New Kingdoms, were defined by kings who ruled a portion of a divided country. So where did this philosophy originate?

The first unification of the 'Two Lands' is a thing of legend and was possibly carried out by King Narmer in approximately 3100 BCE (what is known as Dynasty 0). At this time Egypt was divided into small regions, rather like *nomes*, which were governed by their own chieftains, laws and, to a certain extent, culture.

Unifying these disparate tribal groups would have been a daunting task as it necessitated a number of battles and even laying siege to walled cities until they capitulated. We do not know what the motivation was behind the first unification but it may have developed from a need to utilise the natural resources and therefore required more people to build, maintain and protect earthworks. Centralised earthworks and irrigation required a centralised ruler. Narmer no doubt started small, ruling an area in Upper Egypt and then taking over the communities in close proximity, and as his numbers swelled he expanded his power further afield until he ruled a whole region and then unified the country by taking over Lower Egypt.

This momentous event was recorded on the Narmer Palette. The king is shown wearing the red crown (*deshret*) of Lower Egypt on one side of the palette and wearing the white crown (*hedjet*) of Upper Egypt on the other to demonstrate that he ruled both parts of Egypt. This is why the king throughout Egyptian history is shown wearing what is known as the dual crown, with the white crown inserted into the red crown.

Narmer was the first king to depict himself in what is now known as a traditional 'smiting pharaoh' scene and every king since Narmer depicts himself in this way. He is shown as a smiting pharaoh with the white crown smiting a kneeling enemy – or inhabitant of Lower Egypt – with a mace. No one said the unification was a smooth political event. It was a violent show of strength by this powerful king.

Since the first unification every king of Kemet emulated Narmer in art, in the form of the smiting pose and the wearing of the dual crown of Kemet. Additionally, another common royal motif is the *sm3 t3wy* which is seen on temple walls and statue bases. This scene represents the unification of the two lands and shows two figures, either both of the king, Horus and Seth, or two images of Hapy, the god of the Nile. These

sm3 t3wy symbol on the base of a statue of Ramses II at Abu Simbel.

figures are in the process of tying a papyrus stalk, representing Lower Egypt, and a lotus flower, representing Upper Egypt, around the heart and lungs of Egypt.

Every king aspired to be a dual king and even if they only ruled either the north or south they may refer to themselves as the dual king anyway, even if they were not. But who is going to argue with a king? And generally what is written down becomes the truth for generations to come.

Pyramids

The pyramids in the north of Kemet were already 1,000 years old by the reign of Amenhotep III, and were a popular place to visit for tourists travelling to the north. Unlike the royal tombs built during the reign of Amenhotep III, the pyramids were huge monuments available for all to see and were an awe-inspiring reminder of the power of the king as well as the rays of the sun-god.

The earliest pyramid was the step pyramid of Djoser (2668-2649 BCE) at Saqqara, and was an elaboration of the traditional *mastaba* tomb, a bench-shaped superstructure. It started life with a standard *mastaba* superstructure, with the burial chamber dug 28m below the ground at the bottom of a 7m² shaft. This was part of a complex system of underground galleries and magazines. Once the underground complex was completed the 63m × 8m *mastaba* tomb was built over the top. Just to the east of this *mastaba* were eleven further burial shafts, each 38m deep and each ending in a large burial chamber, intended for Djoser's family. The initial *mastaba* was then extended to cover these extra burial shafts. From this point Djoser decided to continue adding to his *mastaba* tomb, adding a further *mastaba* on top and then another, until there were six of these creating the first step pyramid.

Throughout the next century subsequent kings continued to develop the step pyramid construction, by trying to create a true pyramid. The first attempt at a straight-sided pyramid was made by Sneferu, the first king of the fourth dynasty (2613-2589 BCE) at Meidum. He built a seven-stepped pyramid and started to build up the steps to create a straight-sided pyramid. The top three steps were never covered and gives this monument an unusual appearance.

Sneferu was not a man to give up and moved his monument building to Dahshur, where he made two further attempts at a true pyramid with the Bent Pyramid or 'Southern Shining Pyramid' and the Red or North Pyramid, known as the 'Shining Pyramid'. The Red Pyramid was a success and is second in size only to the later pyramid of Khufu at Giza.

The Red Pyramid was a prototype of the most perfect pyramid and Khufu adopted his techniques to construct his monument at Giza. As Sneferu had put in all the hard work in perfecting the technique all that was left was to make it bigger.

Khufu's pyramid, the Great Pyramid, is the largest pyramid in Kemet at 146m high. The Giza plateau is guarded by the Sphinx, which is

Sphinx, Giza.
(Photograph by
the author).

thought by many to have been built by Khafre (2558-2532 BCE). It has a lion's body and a human face (the face of the king who constructed it). The face of the Sphinx was originally painted a reddish brown with a headdress of blue and gold. The recumbent lion is a symbol of the sun-god and the king's strength and power. This creature is therefore a very powerful image.

Many people in the New Kingdom travelled to Giza to gaze upon this monument to the divinity of the king, and it is known that people slept between the paws of the Sphinx to receive divine messages from the gods.

Uncovering the Sphinx

Between the paws of the Giza sphinx is the Dream Stela of Thutmosis IV (1419-1386 BCE) which stands at 3.65m. The king records how he had fallen asleep at the base of the Sphinx and dreamt that the solar god spoke to him and offered advice on how he could legitimise his claim to the throne. The Sphinx at this time was up to the neck in sand.

> He dreamt in his slumber at the moment when the sun was at the zenith, and it seemed to him as though this great god spoke to him with his own mouth, just as a father speaks to his son, addressing him thus: 'The sand of the district in which I have my existence has covered me up. Promise me that you will do what I wish in my heart; then shall I know whether you are my son, my helper. Go forward let me be united to you.'

Thutmosis IV removed the sand as requested and then when his father Amenhotep II died, he ascended to the throne just as the god had promised.

It was a very peaceful place to visit, some distance away from the city of Heliopolis. There is an element of danger in straying into the desert due to jackals, desert lions and bulls, but the tranquillity and power from being in this divine area was thought to be worth the danger.

Over the years the sphinx became buried by the rising sands, but it was uncovered, and during the reign of Amenhotep III it was possible to get close to this mighty god.

DID YOU KNOW?

There are more than 100 pyramids in Egypt spanning 3,000 years of building, from the third dynasty (2668 BCE) to the eighteenth dynasty (1293 BCE) in both the north and the south of Egypt.

The latest pyramid discovered was in 2017 at Dashur and was dated to the thirteenth dynasty (1782-1650 BCE).

Hyksos

At the end of the Middle Kingdom (1782 BCE) Egypt was hit by a famine which resulted in political upheaval and the division of Egypt, not only into Upper and Lower Egypt but with further divisions within these areas. This period of upheaval was known as the Second Intermediate Period.

During this period the fifteenth and the seventeenth dynasties (1663-1570 BCE) ruled at the same time, with the former in the Delta and latter in Thebes.

Additionally, the fourteenth and fifteenth dynasties ruled simultaneously (1663-1540 BCE). The fifteenth dynasty was known as the *hk3 h3swt*, or Shepherd Kings (*Hyksos*) and despite the propaganda which has circulated since they were chased from Kemet by the Theban seventeenth dynasty, the *hk3 h3swt* were not Asiatic invaders. They took over the throne from within the Canaanite community, which had been settled in the Delta for a century.

The material culture in their capital Avaris (Tell el Da'ba) was a combination of Syro-Canaanite and Egyptian, with an increase in Canaanite culture just prior to the fifteenth dynasty. As the *hk3 h3swt* kings became more powerful more Egyptians moved to the new northern capital, but as time progressed the culture became more Syro-Canaanite. The funerary culture in particular was of Syrian origin, with donkey burials and servant burials, which indicate both were slaughtered at the death of the tomb owners.

hk3 h3swt (Hyksos) traders from the Middle Kingdom tomb of Khnumnhotep III at Beni Hasan. (Picture courtesy of Ulla Kaer Andersen).

The *hk3 h3swt* also worshipped a combination of Egyptian and Canaanite gods with Seth-Baal being the most popular; an amalgamation of the Egyptian god of chaos, Seth, and the Canaanite storm god, Baal. The worship of Seth did not endear them to the people of Kemet as Seth was a dangerous god and not often worshipped by anyone but the bravest kings.

There were six kings which made up the fifteenth dynasty: Shamuqenu (1663-? BCE); 'Aper 'Anat; Sakir Har (1649-? BCE); Khayan Sewoserenre (1649-1609 BCE); Apophis Awoserre/Aqenenre/ Nebkhepeshre (1609-1569 BCE); and Khamudy Hotepibe (1569-1570 BCE). They gained in strength and power as the dynasty progressed.

The *hk3 h3swt* ruled Egypt for ninety years, starting in their Delta capital, Avaris, which was on the Pelusaic branch of the Nile. It was twenty years before they expanded their power southwards, taking control of Abydos, where they waited another thirty years before King Apophis travelled further southwards to try and take control of Thebes. It is thought this final push from Abydos to Thebes took so long due to military intervention of the Theban seventeenth dynasty.

The seventeenth dynasty King, Seqenenre Tao II engaged in a battle with Apophis to try and prevent Thebes being lost to these northern rulers. Seqenenre Tao was killed in this battle and suffered various arrow wounds to the head. He was followed in his quest against the *hk3 h3swt* by his son Kamose, who was able to push them back to Avaris where there was a siege outside the city's enclosure walls.

History is written by the winners and the siege is recorded as a great victory for the people of Kemet. It is recorded by Kamose that: 'I espied his [*Apophis*] women upon his roof, peering out of their windows towards the harbour. Their bellies stirred not as they saw me, peeping from their loop-holes upon their walls like young animals in their holes, saying: "He is swift."'

Kamose was not able to fully complete the campaign against the northern rulers and it is probable that he also died in battle. His brother Ahmose took up the mantle. He was able to chase the final *hk3 h3swt* king, Khamudy – who had taken over the throne following the death of Apophis – out of Egypt. The *hk3 h3swt* were chased as far as Sharuhen in Palestine by the Kemet army.

Ahmose took over the throne of both Upper and Lower Egypt and united Kemet once more, ending the Second Intermediate Period and the era of political instability.

Change in Military Practice

The *hk3 h3swt* takeover introduced long-lasting changes to Kemet although the propaganda texts would have you believe they brought nothing but chaos. The biggest legacy of this period was a change in the military and how the army functioned. In the Middle Kingdom Kemet had a magnificent army but it was on a conscription basis. Very few people chose the army as a career and were simply called up to fight when they were needed. Each *nome* was led by a chieftain who gathered the people required to fight for the king.

However, following the *hk3 h3swt* dynasty a permanent army was introduced and it was possible for young men to forge a military career, working full-time as a soldier, archer or charioteer.

It is a common misconception that the *hk3 h3swt* introduced the chariot to Kemet but this is not, in fact, the case. Both the Egyptians and the *hk3 h3swt* learned the skill of charioteering at the same time, in approximately 1600 BCE. Seqenenre Tao's, and Kamose's army used chariots against the *hk3 h3swt* king, Apophis, in the final battle. Chariots were used at this time primarily to transport soldiers to a battlefield where they would then disembark and fight on foot. However they carried two people – a driver and an archer – so it was possible to fight while moving.

Another change to the military arsenal, which was as a direct consequence of the *hk3 h3swt*, was the composite bow. Traditionally the soldiers of Kemet used the self-bow, which was straight with a slight bend at each end where the bow-string was attached. It was made from a single piece of flexible wood. The composite bow on the other hand was Old Akkadian in style, and had been used in the Near East 700 years prior to reaching Egypt. It was made using small fragments of wood stuck together, providing more flexibility. Rather than being straight, the bow had a dip in the centre where the archer gripped. Furthermore, the composite bow could fire an arrow further, changing the nature of battle. No longer did it have to be fought close up.

The *hk3 h3swt* also introduced the scimitar sword to Kemet as they suddenly appeared after the fifteenth dynasty. They had been popular in Mesopotamia for 700 years before coming to Kemet and were adopted by some Egyptian kings as part of the traditional smiting scenes.

Hatshepsut

The most recent upheaval to the divine equilibrium of *Maat* was the rule of Hatshepsut (1498-1483 BCE). This reign was considered extremely contentious because Hatshepsut – a woman – took over the throne and called herself king. To a resident of Kemet this is confusing, distressing and something that goes against the divine rules of *Maat* and the institution of kingship.

Hatshepsut was the daughter of Tuthmosis I (1524-1518 BCE) and Ahmose, and it is thought that they were brother and sister, an acceptable scenario for royals but not for the ordinary people. Hatshepsut had one full brother, Amenmose, and two half-brothers, Wadjmose and Tuthmosis (II). Amenmose died before he became king, and Wadjmose and Tuthmosis (II) were the sons of a secondary wife of Tuthmosis I.

Tuthmosis I died in year twelve, month nine (1512 BCE) of his reign, leaving the throne to his son, prince Tuthmosis (II). Hatshepsut married him and they had two daughters, Neferure and Neferubity. Tuthmosis II also had another son, Tuthmosis (III), by a secondary wife. Tuthmosis II died in 1504 BCE, leaving Hatshepsut widowed. Thutmosis III ascended to the throne and, as he was only a young child, Hatshepsut married him and they co-ruled. Due to his very young age, Hatshepsut was in complete control of Egypt, initially as a queen.

However, after year seven, she abandoned the queenly titles and adopted the five-fold titulary of a king. She is shown on monuments wearing the masculine attire of a king, including the false beard, and partook in activities normally reserved for kings. For example, she commissioned and dedicated four obelisks at *ipt-swt* (Karnak temple), organised an expedition to Punt in order to bring valuable commodities back to Kemet, and she constructed a tomb in the Valley of the Kings. Once she had taken on the full role of king she bestowed the title of Great Royal Wife onto her daughter, Neferure, giving her the power of queen in a supporting role to her mother as king.

During the first seven years of the co-regency with Tuthmosis III, Hatshepsut filled all the positions of power with loyal men, so when she

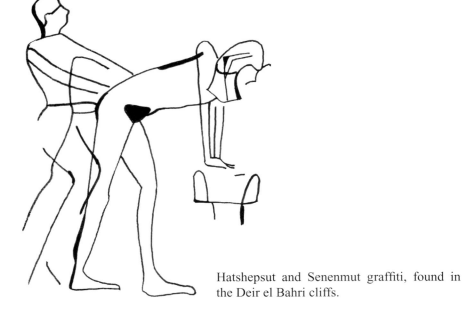

Hatshepsut and Senenmut graffiti, found in the Deir el Bahri cliffs.

declared herself king there was little resistance. The most important of these was Senenmut, the vizier. Some still speculate on the nature of their relationship.

By year twenty-two of the reign, Thutmosis III had regained the throne from his stepmother/wife and once more Egypt was restored to the divine laws of *Maat* with a male ruling as king. Thutmosis III was a strapping man of twenty-five, with a warrior's training and heart, and he was able to restore Egypt to the glory years before Hatshepsut took his throne.

In the later years of his reign the king started destroying the monuments of the female pharaoh, either removing her entirely or replacing her name with his own. Egyptians living after this reign would not have known about this legendary woman because a reign that goes against the rule of *Maat* in this manner was erased from history.

So, now it's time to return to the reign of Amenhotep III in 1360 BCE and learn how, as an outsider to this vibrant city, you could find a job, settle into a new home, set up a family and generally lead a good and fulfilling life.

Introduction to Your New Home

Arriving in Thebes will be daunting unless you have travelled from another large city. Thebes is a vibrant city and the religious capital of Kemet, with the temple of *ipt-swt* (Karnak) being the central hub of royal worship of the god Amun, the local deity. There is more information on religion and the cults of each particular deity in a later section. The first thing you need to do as a new arrival is to get your bearings.

The city of Thebes is separated by the river Nile with – generally speaking – the living occupying the East Bank and the dead occupying the West Bank. Most of the inhabitants live on the East Bank in small villages comprising a series of mud-brick houses clustered together. Temples dedicated to cult deities are also situated on the East Bank.

The West Bank – where the sun sets – is the home of the necropolis and the temples dedicated to the funerary cults of kings past. The main exception to this rule is the village of The Place of Truth (Deir el Medina), which houses the workmen and their families who are responsible for the work on the Valley of the Kings and the royal tombs. This is a walled village and there will be no reason to go here unless you are friends with someone who lives there, or you are lucky enough to be employed on the royal tomb and are invited to live here (see the section on work below).

The palace that His Majesty Amenhotep III built for his queen, Tiye, can also be found on the West Bank to the south and is rumoured to be one of the most beautiful places in Thebes, with a boating lake to rival any other. The palace is called the Palace of the Dazzling Aten, or The House of Rejoicing. It covers a huge area – 30,000m² – and employs hundreds of people. However, this is not a place that can be visited by members of the public as it is surrounded by an enclosure wall preventing any view of the residents inside.

Malkata Lake

To the north of the palace of Malkata was a temple dedicated to Amun, complete with a processional way connected to a T-shaped harbour or lake. This harbour, known as Birket Habu, was 2.5km wide and was connected directly to the Nile by a man-made canal.

The harbour was used as a port for bringing in food and provisions for the palace, but was also used to moor the royal barge, which was known as *The Dazzling Aten*. This golden barge would have carried Amenhotep III and his queen, Tiye on royal river processions.

When the workmen were digging this colossal ceremonial harbour they piled the soil and sand in mounds around the edge of the lake. These mounds can still be seen today where they have stood for 3,500 years.

The only reason most people have for going to the West Bank in general is if they are burying a loved one, taking part in the Beautiful Festival of the Valley (see section on religion below), visiting a tomb of a loved one, or if they are employed in the funerary cult.

Generally, most people spend the majority of their time in Thebes on the East Bank of the Nile. To the south of the city is the *ipt-rshyt* (temple of Luxor) and this is joined to the temple of *ipt-swt* (Karnak), some three miles north, by a processional way, which is covered by a high wall and is not open to the public.

Between these two temples, which, loosely speaking, act as the northern and southern boundaries, is the town of Thebes itself. You are unlikely to find buildings resembling shops or restaurants, although of course individuals will serve food or sell goods from their homes. These will be easy to recognise, especially in the case of butchers or fish sellers, who display their goods outside their home to show what they have to sell. Knowing where the shops are is something you'll get to know once you are resident in the town.

Finding somewhere to live in Thebes will be easier for the expat if accompanied by their family or with the wealth to purchase or build a home.

The majority of the population live in very basic houses, built of mud-bricks made from Nile clay and a roof of tree trunks. It is unusual for a person to live in a house by themselves or for family homes to have a spare room that can be rented out to a new arrival in the city.

The majority of village houses are small, with approximately four rooms, and may measure as little as 40m².[1] And don't be surprised if three generations live there, perhaps as many as twelve people.

In addition to the human inhabitants many households have cats for rodent control, a guard or hunting dog, some ducks or geese (for eggs and later, meat) and goats (for milk). Theban houses are not generally calm, peaceful havens. This is the same for the upper classes, who live in large villas with livestock housed within the open courtyards in the centre. Animals are key to self-sufficiency and a valuable commodity, so the owners keep them close.

It could be difficult, therefore, for a stranger to enter into this family dynamic so it is best to purchase or build a small two-roomed house if you are a sole traveller, or a standard four-roomed house if you are a couple with a young family.

So what can you expect with a standard four-roomed house? The first room in the house leads directly from the street door. This room is often dominated by an enclosed box-bed (see text box) which may be elaborately decorated with images of the lion-headed dwarf god, Bes, and the pregnant crocodile goddess, Taweret.

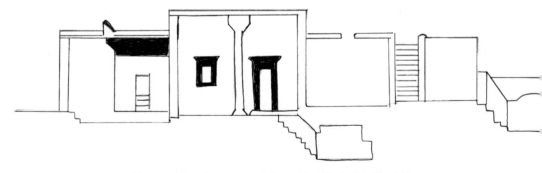

Four-roomed house (drawing adapted from Uphill, 2001, Fig 10).

Box Beds

Box beds are not fully understood as structures, but appeared in homes in both Deir el Medina and Tell el Amarna. They comprised a raised platform made of mud-brick against one wall reached by a couple of small steps. They were enclosed on three sides with a small access opening in the front wall. They may have been roofed, which would have made them dark, claustrophobic structures.

Bernard Bruyère, who excavated at Deir el Medina (1922-1951), believes box-beds were instrumental in the religious cults practiced within the home. Within the box-bed structures themselves a number of clay models of naked women have been discovered, emphasising that female fertility was an important aspect of the function of these structures.

At Amarna they appear to have been used as shrines to the gods Taweret and Bes, and had doors sealing what is thought to be the shrine itself. Both of these deities were closely associated with childbirth and pregnancy.

This connection with fertility and childbirth has led others to suggest box-beds were used as birthing or marital beds although some of them may have been too small for this to be practical.

The first room, being the first that visitors see, is the most visually pleasing. If possible, many people have a column in the centre of the room, or two if they are ostentatious. Columns are a sign of wealth and stone columns are particularly impressive. It is not therefore uncommon for wooden columns to be painted to look like granite to impress the neighbours.

Houses are either long, thin corridors with the second room leading off the first and so forth, or with a square footprint. This all depends on the size of the available land and whether the house has been added to over the years. There is no need for planning permission from a central authority to add to a home; you simply require the land and the means to build.

The second room is often dominated by a large platform used as a seating area during the day and a bed at night. A series of soft furnishings in the form of blankets and pillows can be strewn over this platform for comfort.

As a room intended for family gatherings, ancestors are of course welcome here, and therefore it is traditional to have a false door stela dedicated to a favoured deity or ancestor painted or carved onto the wall. These false doors allow ancestral spirits to enter the house and participate in any activities taking place in this room.

The third room, which leads directly from this family room, is a multi-purpose room utilised according to the needs of the individual family. It can be used as a work area, storeroom or workshop. Workmen use these rooms to create private commissions, or women use them to make clothes or shoes for sale at the market. At night these rooms may be used as a sleeping area for female members of the household, or perhaps a widow could rent this room out to a lone traveller to Thebes (if you are fortunate).

The final room, and without question the most important, is the kitchen, which is normally at the rear of house. It has no roof and has the appearance of a walled courtyard. The clay oven is built against one of the walls and depressions are dug into the floor to stand amphorae jars in. Some courtyard kitchens also have a silo for storing grain, which can be a valuable commodity in time of famine.

Generally, the only natural light in Theban mud-brick houses are small grills in the top of the walls in the first room. The walls in this room are a little higher than those in the other rooms. This means that, at times, houses can get rather smoky with a combination of oil lamps, and the oven being lit. This can lead to a build-up of soot on the walls.

DID YOU KNOW?

Beams in some Amarnan houses were black with smoke from lamps, indicating poor ventilation. This led to a condition called *anthracosis* where soot settles in the lungs, which has been identified in some mummies.

The main difference between these perfunctory houses and the houses of the rich are a combination of extra living space and the addition of a garden where vegetables can be grown. As one would expect, the more expensive the property the better the location. A house can cost between five-sixths of a *deben* of copper or two *deben* of silver; about the same as 200 cubits of rope. The houses of the wealthy often face north in order to take advantage of the cooling northern winds. Obviously this may not always be possible, and if it is not, there will be a corridor leading from the less-than-ideal entrance to a second, north-facing entrance to give the impression to guests that the positioning is perfect.

Large villas can accommodate as many as thirty rooms, which include a columned reception hall, a garden with a small fishing lake and suites of rooms for the women of the house, or for staff and their families.

As a lone traveller, trying to obtain work at one of these villas will secure accommodation as well. Failing that, it may be possible to rent a room, or suite of rooms, in one of these villas, although that depends on the owner and whether this fits into his lifestyle, and the number of unmarried daughters he has. It is unlikely a stranger would be welcomed to live in a house with unmarried girls.

Many rooms in a villa are single-function and even include designated bedrooms for individual residents, some with en-suite water closets. As mentioned above, a standard four-roomed house has to be multi-functional and each room, including the flat roof, is used for family members to sleep at night. Bed-rolls are stored during the day and brought out when needed. By contrast, the bedrooms in larger villas have dedicated furniture in the form of beds with mattresses which stay in place all the time.

Everyone, rich and poor, uses similar head-rests in place of pillows or cushions, made of wood, stone or clay. The quality of the material is, of course, dependent on how much you are willing or able to pay. These are often decorated with images of Bes and Taweret, who protect the sleeper throughout the night from any demons intending to cause harm.

Bedrooms in luxury villas also have stone-lined en-suite shower rooms. These are essentially a stone slab and a shoulder-height wall, behind which a servant stands and pours water over the bather. The waste water drains away through stone channels. Some houses also have a separate water closet with whitewashed walls. Within this room a lavatory is placed, if you are lucky enough to have one, which comprises a u-shaped wooden seat with a bowl of sand underneath. Those not lucky enough to have an inside lavatory have to go outside. Other ablutions are carried out in the Nile or using a bowl of water within the home.

As you can imagine, any inhibitions need to be overcome quickly as personal ablutions, sleeping and living in general are very much done in public. The houses on the whole are small, with numerous people sharing the space, unless you are fortunate enough to secure your own home or a room or suite of rooms in a luxury villa.

Food and Diet

Whenever you go somewhere new the food can be difficult to get used to at first: it tastes different, it is cooked in different ways, different fruits and vegetables are available and the herbs and spices used may not be what you are familiar with. However, consider yourself lucky to be living in the dynamic city of Thebes during the reign of His Majesty Amenhotep. Everything is in abundance and there is a great variety of food to choose from. Even the fussiest eater will find something to tickle their taste buds.

Theban people love to eat. So much, in fact, that when you take your final journey to the west, your tomb – should you be wealthy enough to have one – will have the most sumptuous feasting scenes painted on the walls, with tables piled high with your favourite foods and drink. This ensures you can feast in abundance for eternity. It is boasted about that those who are wealthy even put entire feasts into the tombs for this final journey; all prepared and plated as if for a banquet.

DID YOU KNOW?

The tomb of Tutankhamun contained forty-eight boxes of food, cooked and labelled, twenty-six jars of wine (red and white) and various containers of fruit and vegetables.

Food at Amarna

Scenes from Amarna, the capital city of Akhenaten (1350-1334 BCE), emphasise the importance of food and feasting in the royal household.

Akhenaten was famous for holding regular banquets for his officials as a means of ensuring their loyalty at a time when Egypt was politically unstable due to the religious changes he instigated. These banquets were a luxurious affair and there are various scenes of the royal family eating while seated on elaborate thrones or comfortable cushions.

Not only do we see the food they are eating, which includes cow ribs and whole duck, but also how the royal family ate.

They are seated in a relaxed manner and eat with their fingers, with oil and fat running over their hands and faces. On banquet scenes in other New Kingdom tombs servants can be seen pouring water for the revellers and this could be to remove bits of food from their fingers in the absence of cutlery.

In addition to holding banquets for royal officials, there were also large banquets for religious and state festivals. Often this was a time for the people in the villages and towns to have a day off work. They often received extra food rations, or temples provided a feast for the festival revellers.

But why wait until you are True of Voice (dead)? Enjoy the food now while you are alive. Food is important in Thebes and inviting people to your home for a meal is a regular part of daily life, business life, political life and royal life. People are easily placated by food so it is advisable to find a wife who can cook, or employ a woman to prepare food for you when you want to impress.

So what can you expect to eat in Thebes, and how is it prepared?

Bread

Like all areas of Kemet and the wider world, bread will be a major staple of your daily diet while living in Thebes. However, as there are so many forms of bread, made with different ingredients, you will definitely find one that you really enjoy.

Bread is generally made from emmer wheat or barley, which both have the same name in the language of Kemet: *corn*. The former makes a much tastier bread and it is obviously more expensive than the latter.

The most common bread is flat bread, which is baked on the outside of a hot clay oven. Loaves come in a variety of shapes and sizes and generally the shape of the loaf provides an indication of the main ingredients.[2]

The bread dough is often enriched with fat, milk and eggs making it quite heavy, and enough to fill you if that is all you have for your meal. Other ingredients are sometimes added to the dough for extra flavours; these include olives, fruit or honey. A particular delicacy is a loaf rolled in cumin seeds before baking.

Another delicacy has a layer of mashed dates between two layers of dough, making a wonderful sticky fruit bread. These loaves are cooked inside the oven rather than on the outside and there is a tell-tale hole in the top where they are pushed into the oven with a stick.

To accompany some of the sweet fruit breads it is popular to use a jam made from palm fruit or dates, which can be used to dip the bread into or to spread on top.

The only problem you may find, especially if you hail from a less sandy environment, is that sand and stone dust finds its way into the bread. Whilst not affecting the flavour, this abrasive can be detrimental to your teeth and this is discussed below in the section on health. Unfortunately, there is not an easy way to avoid this inclusion, but if you are fortunate enough to find a baker who makes fine bread then treasure them and return to them daily.

Beer

The water in Kemet is not safe to drink without boiling and straining so a weak beer is produced for daily consumption by everyone, including children. This will become a staple of your diet while in Kemet.

It is made from partially cooked fresh bread. As one would expect, the best bread will make the best beer so keep on the good side of good-quality bakers and brewers. Beer is thick and nourishing and may need to be strained through a sieve before consuming, or drunk through a straw, which prevents the sediment being consumed.

For variety, beer is also flavoured with fruit – mostly dates – or honey, and depending on the time it is left to ferment, can be high in alcohol and can lead to inebriation.

Vegetables

Unless you are particularly wealthy you are unlikely to consume much meat and will survive on a diet comprising fish, fruit and vegetables. This does not, however, mean your diet will be unvaried as the Nile Valley is very fertile. Fruit and vegetables grow in abundance and fish are plentiful in the Nile.

Most families, even those with the smallest piece of land, will grow vegetables to eat, and it would be a good idea in your new home to keep some land for growing the basics. Anything else you need you can obtain from the market or exchange with your neighbours. Kemet is all about community and no single household is expected to be entirely self-sufficient. Being on good terms with your neighbours is definitely advisable.

Many vegetables available in Thebes will be familiar to people from all of the surrounding areas. These include pulses such as lentils, and chickpeas – which are locally called 'hawk-face' due to their shape – hummus and *ful nabed* (broad beans), *ful medames* (fava beans) and *tirmis*. These pulses can be turned into an array of interesting dishes or simply mashed into a paste flavoured with herbs and vegetables and eaten with bread.

One of the most important vegetables in Kemet, from an iconic point of view and as a dietary staple, is lettuce. This is a sacred vegetable associated with the god Amun-Min, the fertility god, and is thought to be an aphrodisiac and an aid to fertility. This is due to the white sap that oozes from the stem of the lettuce when it is cut.

Onions are a great snack and many workmen take these as part of their packed lunch. They are small and sweet and can be eaten without any preparation. As part of a quick and easy lunch, onions are often accompanied with bread and cucumber, all washed down with weak beer.

Other vegetables that you will see at the market when in season are garlic, radishes, leeks, cabbages, cucumbers and celery. Garlic may be different to what you are used to as the heads are quite small but may hold as many as forty-five cloves each. Radishes are white or pink rather than deep red and have very thick roots. They should be cooked in hot water.

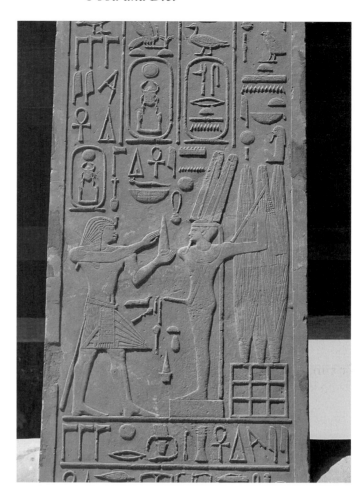

Amun-Min
and his sacred
lettuce, Karnak.

Flavouring

Smell and flavour are very important for the people of the Nile
valley and therefore all of these raw ingredients are brought to life
by using combinations of herbs and spices, which are all available
in the marketplace, such as cumin, coriander seeds, cloves, dill,
lettuce seeds, cinnamon, mustard, mint, fenugreek, rosemary and
wild marjoram. It is possible that you may find olives at the market
although they are generally imported and do not always make it as
far south as Thebes.

DID YOU KNOW?

Akhenaten, the son of Amenhotep III, tried to grow olives at Amarna and there are scenes of him offering olive branches to the god Aten. Funerary wreaths from the eighteenth dynasty also included olive leaves. However, the olive crops in Egypt seem to have been insufficient to press oil and this was considered quite rare throughout the pharaonic period.

Meat and Fowl

As mentioned previously, meat is only for the wealthy, but if you are of the class to read this book then you will probably be able to afford meat, if not weekly then at least on special occasions. It is suggested that the size of the animal you can eat determines the level of wealth you possess, with the king dining on oxen every day and the poorer classes surviving on quail or fish.

DID YOU KNOW?

In studies of the cardiovascular structures of forty-four mummies in 2011, twenty of them had evidence of arterioscleorsis, or the furred-up arteries common with high cholesterol, indicating that those who could afford to eat meat over indulged.

Those with evidence of arterioscleorsis were aged between forty-five and fifty-five years old, whereas those without it were younger. Two of the mummies had evidence of the calcification common with arteriosclerosis in almost every artery, showing an advanced case.

The most common meat available is fowl, and includes wildfowl, ducks, geese, pigeons, egrets, quail and squab; essentially anything that can be caught on the banks of the river Nile. To be honest, if you are handy with a net or even a hunting dog, you could catch these yourselves and eat fowl every day. There are no restrictions on what fowl can be caught and eaten. To prepare, they are generally split in half, flattened and cooked on a grill. Sometimes a bird may be roasted and will be presented with his head tucked under his wing. Pigeon stews are also a popular favourite and can be made with very limited ingredients.

Some families even catch live birds, and rather than eat them straight away, take them home and fatten them up with grain, bread or sweet mash. If you are enterprising enough you could capture a few fowl and start to breed them to sell at market. You will also be able to sell the eggs that the birds produce and these can be used for food.

DID YOU KNOW?

The Harris Papyrus (twentieth dynasty) mentions fattened geese a number of times, indicating that this was common. There are also depictions from many tomb scenes showing animals being force-fed to fatten them up. This is not limited to geese but includes cranes and cattle as well.

Pigs are butchered and eaten by the middle classes, and are a regular meal at the state workmen villages of Amarna and Kahun. Pigs, however, are not offered to the gods and it is unlikely you would see the priests or the king sully themselves by eating pork. Pigs seem to have a bad reputation as many people keep them purely for waste disposal, but when cooked well they can make a tasty dish.

Beef is a lot more expensive and is indeed a rare commodity, except for the elite and royalty. However, none of the animal is wasted. The head is considered a prime offering to the gods and it is a standard image on offering table scenes in temples and tombs to have the head of a cow on the table. Ribs and forelegs are very popular, cooked over the open flames and covered in a delicious sauce.

The offal is often dried and is a cheaper cut of beef, with the liver and the heart considered the tastiest. Ox blood has many uses, including as a remedy for hair loss, or as a tasty and nutritious blood pudding for the whole family.

Even if all you are able to afford are bones you can make a rich stock by boiling in water to be added to vegetable stews, and any fat can be used for cooking. When it comes to beef, whatever you are able to get hold of you can do something with it.

DID YOU KNOW?

In the well-known Pyramid Text known as The Cannibal Hymn there is a section that refers to making stock:

> Their spirits are in the King's possession
> As the broth of the gods
> Which is cooked for the king out of their bones.

In order for meat to last longer in the hot climate we are blessed with in Kemet, it is often dried by placing it in jars of salt or by hanging it in the sun to dry, depending on what is available.

Similar methods are used for meat, fowl and fish. The meat can simply be hung on a wooden rack and left to dry. Fishermen sometimes have racks on their boats and hang them to dry while still on the river. Fowl and meat is dried by placing it in a large amphora jar filled with salt, or pickled in a jar of oil. If these are not options the meat can be buried in hot sand or mud and left to mature for a few days.

There is, however, an unusual relationship between the Thebanites and fish. Although, they form an integral part of the local diet, some fish are considered taboo and banned from being eaten due to the association with the myth of Seth and Osiris. One fish (the *medjed* or Oxyrhnchus fish) is believed to have eaten the phallus of Osiris when his brother killed him, cut him up and scattered his body parts around the country. Although it was forbidden to eat the fish, to catch one was a great symbol of fertility. However, despite these religious associations, fish are not offered to the gods, though they may be offered to the deceased as part of their funerary offerings.

Fish are cooked in a similar way to birds in that they are split down the middle, gutted and cleaned then opened out, flattened and cooked on the grill.

Game

For sporting individuals there is another addition to the table, in the form of game animals caught on desert hunts. The only animals limited to royal hunters are wild cattle and lions. Anything else is available for the agile spear hunter or archer. This can include desert hare, gazelle or oryx.

There are no real restrictions to hunting and, if you have the means to travel to the desert and back, the weapons required and the skill, you can bag as many desert animals as you are able and enjoy a more varied meat diet. See the chapter on sports for more details on this activity.

Cooking Oils, Milk and Cheese

Meat and fish are generally cooked in their own juices and anything left over can be kept for cooking other meals. At the marketplace, however, you may come across as many as thirty different oils for cooking, including sesame oil, almond oil, linseed oil, radish oil and, if you are lucky, olive oil. Each of the available oils will offer different flavour or texture to your cooking.

In addition to fat, other by-products from animals are also commonly used. Thebanites will not waste any part of an animal. So if you know someone who keeps goats, cows or sheep, you can negotiate a fresh supply of milk from them. Milk can be drunk on its own, but it is also used in cooking and to produce cheese. There are two common cheeses available, gebna and labna. Labna is made by straining salty yoghurt into a creamy consistency, and gebna is made from harder salted curds and kept for two or three days to firm.

DID YOU KNOW?

In 2018 it was announced that the oldest cheese in the world had been identified in the Saqqara tomb of Ptahmes, the mayor of Memphis under Sety I and Ramses II. This cheese has aged for an impressive 3,200 years.

The 'solidified white mass' is the oldest solid lump of cheese discovered and analysis shows it was a combination of cow and sheep or goat's milk.

The tomb was originally discovered in 1885, but was lost until it was re-excavated in 2010. This cheese sample was discovered in 2013-14 in a jar, along with a piece of canvas fabric which may have covered the opening. It was discovered in an area to the southern outer wall of the tomb, which seems to have been a storehouse.

Desserts

In addition to having a wide choice of savoury foods with which to cook, there is also a wide variety of desserts to cater to those with a sweet tooth.

For a light after-dinner snack flapjacks or oatcakes are popular and widely available in the market and the villages. They are made with crushed grain, oil or fat, and are sweetened with honey.

Most desserts are date based and bakers who specialise in making them are commonly known as 'workers in dates', showing their prowess with this fruit.

Other fruits are also added to desserts, wine and beer, depending on what is available and can include melons, pomegranates, raisins, and sycamore figs.

The sycamore fig, or wild fig, is small and yellow and has a more astringent taste than ordinary figs, and is religiously significant to the people of Kemet. Many of the richer homeowners will try to grow fig trees in their gardens in order to have a ready supply of this delicious and significant fruit. Cultivating these trees is a tricky job for the gardeners due to the number of baboons that try to steal the fruit.

Lady of the Sycamore

The sycamore fig was the sacred fruit of the goddess the Lady of the Sycamore, an incarnation of the goddess Hathor, Isis or Nut. The Lady of the Sycamore held an important funerary function as she provided figs and water to the deceased in order to ensure they lived for eternity.

She was depicted in two ways, either entirely as a fruit-laden tree, sometimes with arms offering fruit and water to the deceased, or as a woman emerging from the trunk of a tree making offerings. Sycamore figs were often left in the tomb as offerings for the deceased and as a means of showing the presence of the Lady of the Sycamore. Sycamore trees were also planted near tombs to provide the deceased with sustenance and models of leaves were used as funerary amulets.

In chapter 109 of the *Book of the Dead* it describes how sycamore trees of turquoise flank the eastern gate of heaven from which the sun rose every day.

Some fruits like pomegranates are used primarily for flavouring wine and can be quite expensive. They have been grown in Kemet for approximately 400 years, since the time of the *hk3 h3swt* (Second Intermediate Period), as they were always imported from Palestine.

Other fruits, like mandrakes, are for adults only and are used at parties as a narcotic. They can make you feel drunk and happy. Keep out of the way of children as they are toxic if eaten.

Wine

Of course, the most delicious fruit that grows in abundance in Thebes are grapes, which can be eaten, or – and for many this is preferable – made into wine. Thebes is well-known around Kemet for its wine production and some of the best vineyards in the country can be found on the West Bank of the Nile at Thebes. Other areas for growing grapes are Heliopolis, the Delta in the north and the Faiyum.

There are many different quality wines: wine for offerings, wine for taxes, wine for merry making, and a very popular wine called *shedeh*, which is flavoured with spices. Wines can also be flavoured with the dom-palm fruit, which tastes of gingerbread when soaked and is rather pleasant in wine.

The local vineyards are also experimenting in 'blended' wines where different types of grapes are mixed to produce different flavoured wines.[3] Of course, if you are wealthy enough to pay for it, you can also get white wine, which requires each of the grapes to be peeled before the wine-making process is started. It's a very time-consuming job but the wine at the end of it is worth it.

DID YOU KNOW?

Studies carried out on six of the twenty-six jars of wine from the tomb of Tutankhamun by a Spanish team in 2006 show all of them contained tartaric acid, a chemical produced by grapes, and only one jar contained syringic acid, which suggests the wine in this jar was white. This was unusual as red wine was commonly produced in Egypt and white wine is not recorded until the third century AD.

When buying wine, make sure you check the date of manufacture. For the best flavour, wine should be a maximum of one year old. Anything older than this will not be palatable.

Wine Making

The tomb of Nakht in the Valley of the Nobles in Thebes (TT52) depicts the entire process of producing wine, from picking the grapes in the vineyard to storing the wine in jars.

The process starts with picking the grapes, which are then placed into large basins of clay, wood or stone. These basins were plastered with gypsum to make them watertight.

The wine makers step into the basin and tread the grapes to get the juice out. There may have been as many as six men at a time per vat. Above the basin was a wooden frame with hanging straps attached which were used by the men to hold onto while they crushed the grapes. The job of treading the grapes was monotonous, and it is thought someone played a musical instrument to maintain a rhythm and the grape crushers may have sung to pass the time.

The juice from the crushed grapes flowed from the basin via a trough at one end and drained into amphora jars. They were sealed with clay stoppers and labelled with the type of wine and the year of harvest.

Using this method, the mulch from the grapes also ended up in the jar and it was necessary to strain it before drinking. Alternatively, the mulch could be placed onto linen sheets with two poles in each end. These were twisted in alternate directions and all the liquid was squeezed out into a jar. This extra process would make a top-grade wine.

These jars were left to ferment with perforated seals allowing carbon monoxide to escape the jars. The wine was then ready to drink.

Getting a Job

Unless you have wealth by family means, you will not survive long in Thebes without a job, and it is advisable to start looking as soon as you can after you arrive. Finding work as an individual can be very difficult as many positions are passed from father to son for many generations meaning it is not common for vacancies to arise. However, depending on skills and demand, it is always possible to find something to do to earn a salary.

With literacy levels being what they are in Kemet – less than 0.1 per cent – being literate is not relevant when looking for work. There are few jobs which require it, and those that do are well-paid and sought after.

Many positions are personal enterprises rather than large businesses and in this situation if you are unsuccessful in your business then you and your family will not eat. But do not be discouraged as identifying your skills will show what is available to you.

Low-Skilled Roles

There are a number of low-skilled positions which may not pay well but provide a steady income. For example, this could be the role of a laundryman; and they are generally men, even though in the household women are likely to be responsible for laundry. An entrepreneurial laundryman can initially build up a client base by going from house to house offering to do the laundry for a pre-determined price. As a laundryman you will be expected to collect the clothes from the houses – weekly or daily depending on the arrangement – and then wash them in the Nile. The clothes are then returned to the homes the next day.

Most laundrymen are illiterate but they still need to keep records to ensure they know whose clothes are whose. In this situation they keep pictorial records: a picture of a loincloth with three dots next to it will identify that three loincloths were collected, and so on for all the types of clothes collected.

Although satirical in nature with the intention of emphasising the importance of the role of being a scribe, the *Instruction of Dua-Khety* provides a commentary on many other available jobs. This text is well known and people will often quote aspects of it to each other at opportune moments. Of the laundryman it says:

> The washerman launders at the riverbank in the vicinity of the crocodile. I shall go away, father, from the flowing water, said his son and his daughter, to a more satisfactory profession, one more distinguished than any other profession. His food is mixed with filth, and there is no part of him which is clean. He cleans the clothes of a woman in menstruation. He weeps when he spends all day with a beating stick and a stone there. One says to him, dirty laundry, come to me, the brim overflows.

Although not painting the role in a great light, the role of the washerman is a vital one. Middle-class families with large households may not have

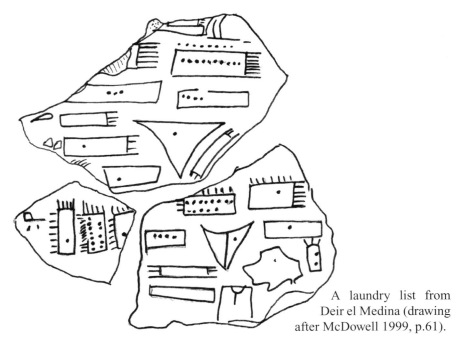

A laundry list from Deir el Medina (drawing after McDowell 1999, p.61).

the time to do their own laundry, and therefore there is potentially a great deal to be gained in this job if you are prepared to work hard. And let's face it, everyone likes to have clean clothes.

Other vital – but often criticised – work is that of the fisherman, which does not necessitate literacy but does necessitate a good work ethic, the motivation to work long hours and the strength for what is hard manual labour. The fisherman is out on his boat at dawn with his partner. One of the fishermen will whack the water with a large stick to encourage the fish to come to the surface while the other casts the net to capture them. Then both men will have to drag the full net onto the boat. They then repeat the process until there is enough fish for the day, either for personal use or for sale.

The *Instruction of Dua-Khety* naturally isn't positive about this role either and states:

> He is more miserable than one of any other profession, one who is at his work in a river infested with crocodiles. When the totalling of his account is made for him, then he will lament. One did not tell him that a crocodile was standing there, and fear has now blinded him. When he comes to the flowing water, so he falls as through the might of God.

However, what Dua-khety fails to understand is the flexibility and potential of this job. If you are wealthy enough to have your own boat you can control how much fishing you actually do, either for your own personal consumption, for a syndicate of people from your village or as a supplier for the market. Things are a little different if you do not have your own boat as you are reliant on someone else who requires help and you will only get a fraction of what is earned from each day's catch.

Soldier

If these jobs don't appeal to you, and you are young, strong and fit then why not join the army. Since the time of the hated *hk3 h3swt* there has been a permanent army in Kemet, meaning young men can start a life-long career in the military working through the ranks. The army is both a career for literate and illiterate young men and can ensure an exciting job.

Literate men can pursue a career as a military scribe, which allows the excitement of battle, but not the danger as you record personnel, itineraries, spoil, prisoners and battle reports. Being a military scribe, however, does not mean you can avoid basic military training, which is gruelling but worth it. As a young recruit you will be subjected to a training regime which includes wrestling, stick fighting, archery and long-distance marching. Some of these activities are discussed in the section on sports. These skills are vital in any battle situation and could save your life.

Once individuals' skills have been identified the recruits are commissioned as charioteers, archers, infantry or scribes. Although being a soldier is a highly prized position, which can be lucrative, battle is not for the faint hearted. It is fought predominantly face to face and involves a great deal of hand-to-hand combat. Unless of course you are an archer. With the recent introduction of the composite bow the archer never has to be closer than 600 cubits (300m) to the enemy, which is a much greater distance than that required with the self-bow. Everyone else, however, conducts battle at a much closer range.

In order to survive battle soldiers must rely on their skills as they do not wear body armour. The protective clothing extends to a linen kilt and a leather over-kilt which is slashed in a criss-crossed manner to facilitate movement. Soldiers fighting with spears will have a shield and those with short swords will have a leather wrist guard as well. Basic sandals (see section on clothes) are made of reeds and frequently need replacing when on long marches.

However, the army are not idle when not fighting in battle. The rest of the time they will be deployed to desert guard posts for weeks or months at a time, ensuring the perimeters of the cities are safe.

DID YOU KNOW?

In the cliffs surrounding the Valley of the Kings a number of simple huts have been discovered which may have provided some shelter for the soldiers who were stationed here to protect the tombs from robbery.

The military were also stationed on the trade routes and desert roads, ensuring safe passage for trade coming into the Nile Valley. In some remote sites the men marked off the days by keeping a tally on the rock face. They were clearly bored on their twenty-day postings and were waiting to return home.

Soldiers are also called upon to help with manual labour when required; for example, clearing irrigation canals following the annual flood or going on expeditions to acquire stone from the quarries in Nubia.

In general, military personnel are well-paid. In addition to a salary when on expedition or at war soldiers get their pick of the spoils of war, which can include anything from precious wood, metals, livestock or even prisoners. They receive land as part of their salary, on the understanding that they can be called up to fight at any time. Once a soldier is too old to fight he will retire, but is permitted to keep the land. This can be farmed and an income generated, ensuring a comfortable old-age. Retired soldiers can also be given honorary priestly titles, which also come with a salary but with no actual work required, thereby providing security in their twilight years. They hold these honorary titles until death. In the wide scheme of things this is an excellent deal as there is no state pension available.

Scribe

If military scribe is too dangerous for you then perhaps use your literacy skills to become a village scribe. This is one of the most coveted positions – at least amongst the middle classes – as it is well-paid, safe and in great demand. With only a very small proportion of society being literate, many people require the services of a scribe for reading and writing letters or asking for advice on legal issues, disputes and dream interpretation. This is considered a very well-thought-of position as Dua-Khety explains:

> As for a scribe in any office in the Residence, he will not suffer want in it. When he fulfils the bidding of another, he does not come forth satisfied. I do not see an office to be compared with it, to which this maxim could relate … It is greater than any office. There is nothing like it on earth. When he began to become sturdy but was still a child, he was greeted (respectfully). When he was sent to carry out a task, before he returned he was dressed in adult garments.

As you can see, the great Dua-Khety admires the position of a scribe greatly. Every major organisation, large palatial home, palace, temple

Amenhotep, Son of Hapu
the scribe of Amenhotep
III, Luxor Museum.

and village has a scribe, with the additional opportunity of working as a
personal scribe for the mayor or local dignitaries. If you are literate there
are indeed plenty of options.

Role of the Scribe

There are extensive records of the work of the scribes from Deir el
Medina, the village which housed the workmen who worked on the
royal tombs in the Valley of the Kings and Queens. These scribes
recorded all the work carried out on the tombs: what went in, what
came out, recording materials, personnel, absentee records, ration
distribution and deliveries into the village.

The scribe then made a report to the vizier, which in turn was
passed onto the king. It would be possible for the village scribe to
make extra income through decorating funerary items with neat,
accurate hieroglyphic and hieratic inscriptions, as well as writing
and reading letters for people in the village.

Messages between Friends

Many messages between friends and family in the village were passed on verbally via a capable child who would repeat the message to the recipient. However, this did not always work out and physical notes were written instead. There are 470 examples of letters from Deir el Medina between friends and family which provide a brief insight into the social lives of the people who lived there. Sadly, the beginning and end of many letters are lost but they cover a myriad of subjects.

This one resorts to writing as the boy who was tasked with delivering the message orally was unreliable:

> Write me what you will want since the boy is too muddled to say it. Look, didn't I write you about it; a fine mat of dried grass and also a fine mat of cord?

Orders for work were also sent by letter:

> 'To the scribe of the Necropolis Hori in life, prosperity, and health, in the praise of your noble god Amen-Re, King of gods, your good lord, every day.
> 'Please send me the plan you will carry out for the painting work.'

There are also letters covering difficult subjects like adultery, and this letter is from wife to her husband:

> 'I, did not take you aside to say, you should look to what you will do about your wife! And to say, you are blind about her! You have kept me from deafening you. The crime is the abomination of Monthu! Look, I will make you see this continuous fortification which your wife committed against you!'

The husband replies:

> 'But she is not my wife? She finished making her speech, and she went outside leaving the door open.'

Learning to Write

In ancient Egypt when training a scribe to write they were first taught how to write in hieratic and then if they were adept at that they progressed onto hieroglyphs.

In the modern world we start the Egyptian language through the study of hieroglyphs and then a small proportion of scholars go on to study hieratic. The complete opposite to the ancient method of literacy.

So what is the difference between hieratic and hieroglyphs? Hieroglyphs are the beautiful texts that are seen on temple walls and comprise detailed pictures which form a phonetic language. This was solely used in religious contexts – so tombs, temples and religious artefacts.

Hieratic on the other hand was the everyday script used by scribes for administration, literature and secular texts. It was a shorthand version of hieroglyphs and is affected more by handwriting than hieroglyphs and is therefore more difficult for a modern scholar to learn. The best thing about hieratic though, is that unlike hieroglyphs it is sometimes possible to identify the exact scribe who wrote the text.

Priesthood

Another career path, which has also recently been introduced, is that of the priesthood. No longer are priests on a three-month rota system with everyone working at the temple for one month at a time, returning to their families after the month is over. Now there are opportunities for a full-time career in addition to the traditional part-time option.

This career is open to everyone. It is not considered to be a post of religious vocation, although some may enter it due to a deep faith. For many, working at the temple, regardless of the level of position, ensures being well-fed, clean and dressed in fresh linen every day. Additionally, the work is not hard compared to the unskilled labour of a farmer or fisherman.

As you have settled in Thebes the ideal temple to get work in will be *ipt-swt* (Karnak temple) and there are thousands of staff members there so this may not be so difficult to achieve.

The Priesthood of Amun at Karnak is divided into five ranks with the first prophet being the highest rank and fifth prophet being the lowest. Second and first prophet are the highest positions in the temple and are reached through personal ambition and political or royal favour. They have a good salary, power within the temple and politically, and are provided with accommodation and land.

If you are hoping to get a role as a prophet you will need to start in the position of fifth prophet and work your way up. It is easier to reach the position of first prophet in a smaller temple, of which there are many in Thebes and the surrounding villages, so it is all dependent on personal ambition.

However, within the lower ranks of the priesthood there are numerous other available roles, depending on the skills you may have. The lower clergy is known as *wab*, or purification priests, and play an important role, including the carrying of the sacred barque, cleaning the temple, and supervising the painters and draftsmen. Anyone – part-time or full-time – can enter the priesthood at this level.

Other low-level priests who hold an essential role are stolist priests, or 'Priests of the Loincloths', as they are more commonly known. They are concerned with the toilette of the divine statue and their role includes dressing the statue, adorning the statue with jewellery, anointing perfume and looking after the ritual materials. To actually touch the divine statue is a privileged job and not one you can step into straight away. You will have to prove your worth before being allowed to get close to the divine statue.

If you are literate there are opportunities in the House of Life, which is an archive and place of learning within the temple where all religious texts are written, restored and archived. In addition to Priests of the House of Life, there are also Teachers of the House of Life, with opportunities to impart skills of reading, writing and religious texts to the younger generation if you have a talent for it.

House of Life

The works of the House of Life (*per-ankh*) were greatly respected around the ancient world and Greek and Latin texts praise the wisdom to be found there. It was reputed to contain knowledge of medicine, medical herbs, geography, geometry, astronomy and the history of kings. Sometimes Greek travellers accredited The House of Life with containing sacred theological knowledge. Egyptian priests were known to have imparted information to the Greeks when they travelled to Egypt.

Strabo records that the true year was unknown to the Greeks until it was translated from the Egyptian priests' writings into Greek, indicating that the House of Life also had detailed astronomical charts.

Egyptian texts also make reference to the House of Life and what is stored within. In the famine inscription at Sehel, for example, the king asks the lector priests about the location of the dwelling of Hapy, god of the Nile Inundation. The priest responds that he will consult the books from the House of Life: 'I shall enter the *per-ankh*, unroll the scrolls of Re, I shall be guided by them.' The information on these scrolls revealed all the knowledge required to stop the drought causing the famine.

The Late Period story of Setne explains that should a particular text be read from the *per-ankh*, it will enable the reader to understand the secrets of the Universe, as well as possessing the ability to understand what the birds and fish are saying. Additionally, some parts of the text will enable them to see the sun god Re in the sky. This was clearly a very powerful text, and would have been stored in the safety of the House of Life to prevent it from getting into the wrong hands.

Another role that also ensures a steady career is that of funerary priest (*sem* or *ka* priest) who is responsible for carrying out the rites and rituals on a dead body before burial. These include prayer recitations, water sprinkling, lighting of incense, and the Opening of the Mouth ceremony (see section on religion below). One would need a strong constitution for this role as it involves being in the presence of dead bodies every day or being in the tombs administering to the cult of the deceased.

Djekhy's Business

An archive of texts dating from between 675 BCE and 590 BCE – a little later than the setting for this book – has provided a wonderful insight into the lives of a family of *ka* priests who were known as *choachytes* at the time. *Ka* priests maintained the cult of the deceased by leaving offerings and saying prayers for the deceased at the tomb chapels on the West Bank.

Djedkhonsuiufankh, known as Djekhy, and his son, Iturech, were *ka* priests in Thebes and were responsible for carrying out rituals and making offerings to the dead on behalf of others, for a fee. This fee often took the form of land which was then rented out to others, providing a regular income.

The archive records the details of their business transactions as funerary priests. One document discusses another priest, Petosiris, son of Iturech, and two other men who were spreading the news that he had been commissioned to service a new tomb in the Theban Necropolis. However, this tomb was already a 'client' of Djekhy and his colleagues. Therefore, the author considers this as a 'hostile takeover'. After raising this problem, Petosiris had to relinquish any claim on the tomb, passing it back to Djekhy and his colleagues. He then had to file an oath before the god Khonsuemwasneferhotep to say he agreed to the terms.

Another document deals with Iturech's acquisition of two new 'mummies' to perform funerary rites for. Iturech and a partner, Khausenmut, signed a contract to split the role; half the practices and half the payments each. These new mummies brought the recorded 'clients' of Irutekh to four, perhaps five.

Death really was a commodity for this family.

Jobs for Women

Although the majority of this advice is aimed at men looking for work, women are not excluded from employment. Jobs for women are, however, a little harder to come by. Women generally have the role of 'Lady of the House' where they take care of the home and the children. Additionally, they carry out home industries such as dress-making, sandal-making or making food to sell at the market. Anything that can be carried out in or near the home while accompanied by young children is carried out by women. This includes winnowing, gleaning and grinding grain during harvest time. However, even if employed, a woman must still carry out her household tasks.

It is not unheard of for a skilled woman to hold administrative positions in large households. It would, however, be preferable in this scenario that she is without a family. So an unmarried woman could secure a position in a private house, such as treasurer, superintendent of the dining room, or sealer responsible for sealing boxes, rooms and letters on behalf of the householder; a position of great responsibility.

Women generally work in the service of other women and are not allowed to oversee the work of men. It is, however, possible for women to oversee the work in female departments of the royal palace, such as Mistress of the Royal Harem, Overseer of the Wig Shop, or Overseer in the House of Weavers. It is unlikely that a married woman could secure a job in the palace as such an important role would entail having to live in the palace rather than the village.

The majority of women, therefore, do not have the privilege of working in the palace and may instead enter industries such as the linen trade. Women can also enter the priesthood and make a good career out of it. Priestesses, like priests, can either be full-time or work one in four months on a rotation system.

Women generally work in cults of goddesses such as Neith and Hathor more than cults dedicated to gods. However, due to the size and diversity of Karnak temple, there are jobs there for priestesses despite being dedicated to a male deity. It may also be easier for a woman coming to Thebes from the outside to gain temple employment as, unlike the male priesthood, the female priesthood is not passed down from generation to generation.

Whereas the primary role of a priest is to care for the statue of the god, the role of priestesses is different. Many roles, such as chantress, songstress or musician, are concerned with processions and worship. They participate in daily rituals of the temples, but much of their role is secret and disclosed only to those who are admitted to the temple. These roles are generally held by wives of the middle classes and having a family does not affect the role.

Midwife

Not all jobs for women necessitate leaving the family and village. These are varied depending on available skills. One of the most lucrative roles is that of midwife, and most villages will have one. Depending on the number of women of child-bearing age in the village, there may be room for more than one and a city the size of Thebes can certainly accommodate a number of such talented women.

Midwifery skills are generally learnt through experience by assisting the village women, and the vast majority of midwives receive no formal training. An entrepreneurial woman who is young enough could approach the village midwife and ask to train with her. The pay for this role is not stable, however, and each midwife will get paid whatever the village women can afford, which naturally will vary. Needless to say, a good and active midwife is not likely to go hungry, but she is unlikely to be rich.

Wet Nurse

Now, if your wife has just given birth and is still nursing the child, she could consider working for the upper classes as a wet nurse. Many upper-class

Hathor nursing the king, Edfu.

families hire local village woman to nurse the children, and it is possible that she could nurse more than one child at a time and therefore earn more.

Wet-nursing is potentially a long-term role. Each child in Kemet is nursed for approximately three years as it is the easiest way of ensuring uncontaminated food for the child. Wet-nurses are guaranteed to be fed well and looked after by their employer as it ensures the health of the babies she nurses.

Mourner

Another role that is open for women only is that of professional mourner. They are hired for royal and noble funerals to throw dust over their heads, render their clothes, scratch their cheeks and wail in grief. It is considered unseemly for women of the deceased's family to display publically such grief but mourners are expected at a funeral, so women and young girls are hired for the occasion.

Professional mourners, tomb of Khaemhat, Valley of the Nobles, Thebes.

Wages

Wages are generally paid on a monthly basis for government work – such as workers at the Place of Truth (Deir el Medina) – and will be in the form of rations in the absence of a monetary system. Rations are primarily paid in grain but can also include fish, vegetables, water, wood for fuel, pottery for household use and clothing. In general, wages provide enough grain to feed a large family, plus a little more, which can be used as currency to exchange in the market for goods not provided by the rations.

In addition to standard rations, government workers also receive bonus rations on festival days or other special occasions. These include sesame oil, blocks of salt, natron and even cuts of beef.

Strikes

The workmen of Deir el Medina were supposed to get paid their rations on the twenty-eighth day of each month, but on many occasions these were late. In year twenty-nine of Ramses III, delays in the delivery of rations had been going on for six months, resulting in the workmen going on strike, with sit-down protests before the funerary temples of Thutmosis III, Ramses II and Sety I.

One text describes this event:

> It is because of hunger and because of thirst that we come here. There is no clothing, no ointment, no fish, no vegetables. Send to pharaoh, our good lord, about it and send to the vizier, our superior that sustenance may be made for us.

On this occasion they received their rations, but later that same year Djhutymose, a scribe from Deir el Medina, went with two bailiffs to collect the grain himself from the local farmers and the temples, as the rations had once again not arrived.

Obviously as you would expect, wages vary according to position and skills. So what can you expect to earn in some of the most common roles at the Place of Truth (Deir el Medina)?

- Foreman or scribe – 7.5 sacks of corn a month worth fifteen *deben*
- Worker – 5.5 sacks of corn a month worth eleven *deben*
- Gatekeeper or Physician – 1.5 sacks of corn a month worth three *deben*

Each sack holds about seventy-seven litres of grain and can be exchanged for other goods in the market.

Other roles may have a daily pay rate and many people are living on the bare minimum of ten loaves of bread a day and two jugs of beer. There is a lot of poverty in Kemet but there is little to no waste. Everything you have will be used and reused until it no longer has a purpose.

Beliefs and Rituals

One thing you will notice when you arrive in Thebes, and indeed Kemet in general, is that religion plays an important part in everyday life. Almost every aspect of life in Egypt is governed in one way or another by the belief in gods and the associated mythology. For example, the river Nile, which is vital to survival in the Nile Valley, is believed to start flooding every year due to a single tear from the eye of the goddess Isis who weeps for her murdered husband Osiris. This is celebrated annually on the 'Night of the Tear', which not only celebrates the start of the inundation but also honours Isis as a nurturer and the life-giving function of the Nile. Clouds in the sky are believed to be the bones of the god Shu, and the sweet north wind is the invisible presence of the god Amun.

One of the most public elements of religious beliefs are the religious festivals which take place, and in Thebes there are sixty-five festival days a year. This provides opportunities for people to meet, dance, sing and feast together. It won't be long after you arrive in the city before there is a festival for you to enjoy.

The most important festivals are the Opet Festival and the Beautiful Festival of the Valley, which will be discussed below. The New Year celebration on day one, month one of the Season of the Flood is an important one and greets the start of the flood season, as well as celebrating the birthday of the sun-god Ra-Horakhty. On day fifteen of the same month offerings are made to Hapy, the Nile god, and the Theban god Amun, to ensure a good flood. These are both important festivals and worth participating in if you get the opportunity.

In month one of the Season of Sowing are the sailing festivals, which see lots of activity on the Nile and are an amazing sight. On day twenty is the sailing of Wadjyt (the eye of Horus), on day twenty-nine is the sailing of Bastet (the cat goddess) and the festival of Raising the Willow, followed by the sailing of Mut, Lady of Isheru (the wife of Amun) on day thirty.

In month two of the Season of Sowing is a festival which lasts for a number of days, starting on day thirty. This 'midwinter' festival takes place in the middle of the year and is known as the 'Amun-in-the-festival-of-raising-heaven', during which, branches of the ished-tree – sacred to the sun-god at Iunu – are brought to the temples. The next day is the first day of a new month and this is celebrated in a ceremony known as 'Filling the sacred eye in Iunu'.

Day eleven, month one of summer sees the festival of Min, the ithyphallic fertility god. This is a four-day festival celebrating fertility and is held at the New Moon. Exactly how you celebrate a fertility festival can be left to your own discretion.

Temples

Thebes is also home to enormous temples like *ipt-swt* (Karnak) temple and *ipt rshyt* (Luxor temple), but what surprises many non-Egyptians is that these temples are closed to the public. The only people allowed inside are the king, the priests and temple workers. However, on specific days members of the upper classes may be allowed to go into the first courtyard to dedicate a statue to the gods. If you know someone with access to the temple you can always ask them to dedicate a statue for you or take offerings into the temple, but be prepared to pay for this service, even if they are a friend.

Ipt-swt (Karnak) and *ipt rshyt* (Luxor temple) are closely connected and it is said there is a beautiful sphinx avenue which joins the two temples, but this is screened off from public view. There are, however, a number of public processions that travel through the streets, rather than taking the sphinx avenue, enabling the public to see the barque of the god housing the god's spirit inside the statue. This can be very inspirational even if you cannot actually see the statue itself. It is the closest most people will ever get to the gods.

These public processions are a splendid spectacle with priests dressed in the brightest, white linen kilts, carrying incense burners, throwing balls of resin into the fire every few steps and filling the air with the scent of Amun. The priestesses and chantresses follow, singing and dancing, giving praise to the god. The barque with the sacred shrine of the god will be carried upon the shoulders of the priests and though the statue is not visible to the public lining the streets, simply being in the presence of the god, whose *ka* resides in the statue, is enough to receive the blessings.

The biggest festival in Thebes is the Opet Festival, which lasts an incredible twenty-seven days, from day nineteen of the second month to day twelve of the third month of Akhket (the inundation season, from mid-August to September). This is a celebration of the union between the king and Amun, and the king leads a procession in which the Shrine of Amun is carried from the sanctuary at *ipt-swt* (Karnak) to visit the harem at the Temple of the Southern Opet (*ipt rshyt*, or Luxor Temple).

Resplendent priests with bald heads and bright, white linen kilts carry the barque to the quay at *ipt-swt* (Karnak) and then on a gold-plated barge to carry him south to *ipt rshyt* (Luxor temple). Along the riverbank worshippers follow, and this could be a great place to view the procession if it is your first time. There is an elaborate procession including drummers, lute players, dancing girls doing back flips, blind harpers, priestly singers, army units, wrestlers, charioteers and the entire entourage of temple priests.

Such a big festival as the Opet festival will often see extra rations distributed to the workforce, which is obviously a cause for extra festivities within the villages.

Extra Rations

The extra rations provided to the villagers of Deir el Medina for the Opet Festival during the later years of the reign of Ramses II was recorded by the village scribe, Anupemheb. He records 150 donkey-loads of provisions brought to the village of approximately seventy homes (covering an area of 5,600m²). This load included:

- 9000 fish
- Ten oxen ready for slaughter
- Four donkey-loads of beans and sweet oils

- Eight donkey-loads of barley malt – enough for four pints of beer each
- 9000 loaves of bread – 150 per household
- Eight donkey-loads of natron (used as soap)

All of this extra food was in addition to the standard monthly rations and was enough for twenty-four days of feasting for a family.

Another important festival – some eight months after the Opet Festival – is the Beautiful Festival of the Valley, where the statue of Amun is carried in procession from *ipt-swt* (Karnak temple) to the necropolis on the west. This ithyphallic form of Amun-Re visits the temple of *Djeser Djeseru* (Deir el Bahri) and 'spends the night' with the goddess Hathor.

He spends two days visiting the royal funerary temples on the West Bank to join the resident gods for rituals and offerings.

For the river crossing from the east to the west bank the sacred barge is pulled by another boat with oars steered by the king and the high priests. There is also often a flotilla of vessels of all shapes and sizes in order to enable the populace to participate in the festival.

Married couples also use this time to invoke blessings on their sexual relationships and associate themselves with the divine couple (Amun and Hathor). Couples sleep at the Hathor shrine on this night and hope to receive a dream of the goddess, which will answer all of their petitions. It is also thought that having intercourse at this time results in conception.

State gods

In the same vein as the state temples being closed to the public, the state gods, while worshipped and honoured by the public, are not their main deities of choice. The gods Amun or Ra are more concerned with the activities of the king than a normal villager. But don't fret, there are dozens of household gods that are worshipped in the homes of the populace, who focus directly on their daily concerns.

Worship in the Home

Most families have a shrine in their homes, normally in the first room of the house. These vary in size – depending on the size of the home – and bear statues of the deities favoured by the members of the household. Depending on the needs and role of the people of the house, the deities worshipped there will be different.

The daily worship is very similar to that in the temple, but without the need of a priest to officiate. Every morning the statues are washed – providing they aren't made of unfired clay – redressed if they are clothed, and provided with nourishment, food and beer. Once the deity has received spiritual nourishment from the food offered, the food is then distributed to the family and passes on blessings and benefits from the connection with the god.

Ptah

Gods worshipped in the home are often connected with household interests such as health, childbirth and fertility. Some of the deities are state deities but with a household slant. For example, the state creator god Ptah is very popular at the workmen's village, the Place of Truth (Deir el Medina), as he is the patron deity of craftsmen. In state religion Ptah is a creator god, responsible for creating the world through words alone.

The workmen on the royal tombs have to work in dark, enclosed spaces that are filled with dust and smoke from the lamps. It is therefore not surprising that many workmen suffer with problems with their eyes or even full blindness. Many attribute the cause of these eye problems not to working conditions but to the displeasure of the god Ptah. Ptah is particularly sensitive to blasphemy and it is thought that 'swearing falsely by Ptah' will 'cause me to see darkness by day and be like the hounds of the street.'[4]

Hathor

Another state deity worshipped in the home is Hathor, the goddess of love, fertility and motherhood. As a state goddess, she is believed to be the mother of the king. In the home, however, Hathor is worshipped – not really surprisingly – in her form as goddess of sexuality and motherhood.

In chapter 148 of the *Book of the Dead* Hathor takes the form of the Seven Hathors and one of her roles is to pronounce the fate of a new-born baby. Along with the Bull of Heaven, the Seven Hathors also provide sustenance for the deceased and ensure that Hathor has a role in both life and death. Her other role in the afterlife is as 'Goddess of the Western Mountain' where she is shown as a cow leaving the desert and emerging through the marshes. This shows she offers a link between death and the Western Desert and the living Nile.

Hathor had a major sanctuary at Memphis dedicated to her in her role as 'Lady of the Sycamore' who provides sustenance for the deceased in the afterlife in the form of sycamore figs (see the section above on food).

In Thebes, however, her main role is as the goddess of love and beauty. In addition to being worshipped in household shrines, the Hathor temple at *Djeser Djeseru* (Deir el Bahri) is open to the public at certain times. It is common for people to travel to the Hathor shrine and leave offerings

Seven Hathors, temple of Ramses III at Medinet Habu.

to her in the hope she will bless them with fertility. These offerings can take the form of clay phalli, which you could commission or fashion yourself, or, alternatively, figurines of nude women with their genitalia and breasts emphasised. If these are not within your budget, Hathor (the 'Golden') is kind and gentle and will accept beads, jewellery, or amulets; preferably something personal. As long as the offerings are left with conviction Hathor will answer your prayers.

Hathor also has male followers too. They do not necessarily appeal to her for the same reasons, but for issues associated with male sexuality, such as infertility and impotence.

The lighter side of Hathor is as the 'Lady of Drunkenness' and the Deir el Medina festival of Amenhotep I, which is celebrated every two months, is seen as a very good time to get drunk. The festival comprises 'four solid days of drinking together with their children and wives.' The Festival of Drunkenness is to appease the lioness form of Hathor, Sekhmet. According to legend, Sekhmet was on a rampage to kill mankind for turning against the sun-god Ra. The priests distracted her by filling the river with beer and dying it red to trick her into thinking it was blood. As the story goes:

> When the maidservants were bruising the grain for making beer, these mandrakes were placed in the vessels which were to hold the beer, and some of the blood of the men and women who had been slain. Now they made seven thousand vessels of beer.

She drank it all and fell into an inebriated sleep and when she awoke she no longer wanted to go on her murderous rampage:

> And the Majesty of Ra spoke concerning this goddess, saying, 'Let there be made for her vessels of the beer which produce sleep at every holy time and season of the year, and they shall be in number according to the number of my hand-maidens.'

Other festivals dedicated to drunkenness include Tekh, which takes place on day twenty of month one of the Season of the Flood. This is then followed two days later by the Great Procession of Osiris.

Bes

The most popular household god is Bes. He can be rather startling to those who are not used to such mixed iconography in a deity. He is depicted with a lion's head and tail and bears the body of an achondroplastic dwarf, with bowed legs and his feet turned outwards. He has a distended stomach and prominent buttocks and is one of the few gods depicted face on, rather than in profile.

Sometimes as a variant Bes' lion's tail is replaced with a full lion pelt draped over his shoulders, like a cape, or he has a pair of wings

Bes, Denderah.

emerging from his shoulder blades. This little god is also shown playing a drum or tambourine and dancing. He often carries the *s3* symbol – a sign of protection – as well as a large knife. He clearly is a versatile little chap.

So why would anyone worship him? He has a number of roles, generally associated with fertility, childbirth, and protection of new-born babies. He is therefore popular with pregnant women and new mothers.

Midwives call upon 'The Good Dwarf' for protection when they are birthing a child and in his role as Aha, The Fighter, he is shown on birthing wands to protect the new mother during this extremely dangerous time. This role has a dangerous and violent nature which scares away demons who would do harm.

Similar representations of Bes bearing a knife can be found on headrests, showing that while you sleep away the hours of darkness he will protect you by scaring away anything malevolent, be they evil demons or disgruntled ancestors (see ancestor cult below). New mothers will also use furniture which is decorated with images of him, and amulets made into pendants and bracelets are very popular all over Kemet. They are generally worn by pregnant women, but also on the necks of new-born babies to offer them the same protection.

Taweret

Bes is worshipped alongside the pregnant hippopotamus deity, Taweret, who is also a protector of pregnant women and new-born children. She appears on the same class of objects as Bes: birth wands, beds, headrests and amulets.

Taweret is a rather terrifying figure and is depicted standing upright on her hind legs, with the head of a hippopotamus, the four limbs and paws of a lion, a mane in the form of a crocodile's tail, pendulous human breasts and an abdomen swollen with pregnancy. She carries the *s3* sign of protection, an *ankh* representing eternal life, a knife or a torch, the flame of which repels evil spirits, demons or hostile dead.

She is also closely associated with Hathor and can be depicted wearing the cow horn and the sun-disc headdress common to Hathor.

Ancestor Cult

The most prevalent home worship is that of your own family ancestors. The idea behind this, in a nutshell, is that upon death and, more importantly, rebirth, the deceased becomes a demi-god, known as an *akh ikr en re* or Excellent Spirit of Re. They are not as powerful as a full deity, but are more powerful than a human. They are able to interfere – both positively and negatively – in the lives of humans but also interact with the gods of the afterlife. Therefore, it is believed by the people of Kemet that a family member is more inclined to help with personal issues if they are within their power.

Generally, the ancestor worshipped in a home is no more than two or three generations past – within living memory of someone within the home – and more often than not the ancestor is a woman. There is no hard and fast rule as to why this is; it is just a convention that seems to be followed.

As a focus for the worship, a very generic statue known as an ancestor bust is placed within the household shrine. They are small, little bigger than a cubit but often smaller. They show only the head and shoulders, with a wig clearly defined, and sometimes the outline of a collar. Of course, when dealing with personal deities, and in particular family members, there are variants; if you wish to honour your uncle who was gloriously bald then there is no protocol preventing the ancestor bust being made in his image. The material used to produce ancestor busts also varies according to personal finance; they can be carved from wood, faience or clay. Sometimes the face is painted, or left to show the natural material.

As the ancestor will be familiar to the family, there is little need for an identifying inscription. The faces are also not intended to be portraiture, and this makes it easy for an ancestor bust to be used for many generations, with the identity of the bust changing as ancestors fall out of living memory.[5]

Some families will also commission an *akh ikr en re* stele to be made in honour of an ancestor to be worshipped alongside the ancestor bust. They are small, generally smaller than half a cubit. They depict a named ancestor who is often seated and holding a lotus flower. Sometimes a servant or living member of the family is shown making offerings to them in order to appease them or honour them. A small number of them may have the deceased ancestor making an offering to a god, either Anubis or Re-Horakhty. As they are for personal worship, there are very few guidelines that need to be followed in regard to their production and use.

So what do you do with the ancestor bust and little ancestor stela? In the home they are generally the focus of offerings of food and drink – as with any other deities – but they are more likely to answer petitions and offer favours to members of the household. These requests could be for children, for help with a neighbour, to help with a false accusation, or even to ask the ancestor to put a good word in with the deities of the afterlife to smooth your path to rebirth.

During the Beautiful Festival of the Valley (see above), the people of Thebes can accompany the procession of the divine statue of Amun to the cemetery on the West Bank with their ancestor busts. This enables the ancestors to be part of this very important and spiritual celebration. Often the procession includes the public, musicians, dancers, soldiers and anyone else who wants to participate in celebrating their families and their ancestors' lives.

The families then feast with the ancestors at the tomb chapel or tomb. Food is laid out on pottery dishes and the dead will take spiritual

Procession of dancers, Red Chapel of Hatshepsut, Karnak. (Photograph by the author).

Funerary banquet, tomb of Paheri, El Kab.

nourishment from it, at the same time as the living are receiving physical nourishment from it. If there is a particular request to one of the deceased ancestors some literate families may write a letter to the dead on the bottom of one of the dishes that is piled high with food. Once the deceased has taken nourishment they will notice the letter and be obliged to answer in payment for the food received.

Letter to the Dead

The Qaw bowl was discovered in tomb 7695 at Qaw and was placed behind the head of the deceased. It had a letter from Shepsi to his mother Yi written on the outside of the bowl. It is dated to the late Old Kingdom to First Intermediate Period and is currently in the Petrie Museum at University College London.

It is Shepsi speaking to his mother Yi:

This is an oral report concerning you saying to her son (i.e. the speaker): "You shall bring me poultry so that I can eat it," and when your son brought seven quails you ate them. Shall one act against me in your presence, so that my children are unhappy and your son is suffering? Who will pour water for you?

O, may you judge between me and Sobek-hotep.

I have brought him from another city in order for him to be laid to rest in his burial place and to be given mortuary garments.

Why is he acting against your son so unjustly, although there is nothing I have done or said. Hurtful is evil committed against the gods.

Shepsi, in this letter, reminds his mother that he brought her quails to eat at her request, and is asking her to intervene between him and Sobek-hotep. Sobek-hotep is deceased and Shepsi is concerned that he is working against him from the afterlife. Perhaps Shepsi has had a run of bad luck and blames Sobek-hotep for it.

Oracles in Processions

As mentioned above, processions are a staple worship practice in Thebes and during your time here you will witness processions of statues, boats, the military and, if you are very lucky, a procession with the king himself.

As well as being a wonderful public spectacle and an opportunity to meet friends and family in celebration, there is also a serious element. Processions bearing the statue of a god can also be approached as an oracle.

Oracles are a means of asking for the god to pass judgement on any matter of concern. Often they take place within a temple complex, where the problem is written on an ostraca[6] and left with the priests at the temple who present it to the shrine bearing the statue of the god. The answer is determined by casting lots with straws or twigs.

In a procession the oracle works a little differently as potentially the petitioner can address the deity in his shrine directly, although it is preferred that the petition is posed through a priest. The statue in the shrine is carried upon the shoulders of a number of priests. In answer to the question the statue will force the bearers to move in a certain way; for example tipped forward for yes, tipped back for no.

There is an incident from the Place of Truth (Deir el Medina) which has gone down in legend where the draftsman Kaha petitioned the god about some clothes that had been stolen. He listed all of the people in the village and when the house of the Scribe Amennakht was recited the god made it clear that the clothes were, in fact, with the daughter of Amennakht. There was little doubt in anyone's mind that he was the guilty party and some even say they heard the god speak and announce the guilty party. Many Thebanites use this anecdote to prove the effectiveness of the oracle.

Pilgrimages

Thebanites are very keen on taking pilgrimages and this is something you will hear a lot about. You may even consider participating in one, even though you may only just have arrived in Thebes. The most important pilgrimage is to Memphis, the site where the god Ptah created the world simply by thinking and speaking his desires.

Another important pilgrimage site is Abydos, which is the burial place of the Lord of the Underworld, Osiris. This pilgrimage is made by young and old alike, although the elderly feel a greater pull as it is seen as a place where an individual's chance of eternal life is enhanced by their close proximity to Osiris. Traditionally, this journey was taken by the funerary barge as part of the funeral. The funeral procession was met at the Abydos necropolis by a priest and a group of traditional *muu* dancers. In reality, however, this pilgrimage is today carried out as a dummy trip from the east bank to the west bank of the Nile without actually travelling to the burial place of Osiris. As long as the same rituals and prayers are carried out it should be enough to simulate a trip to Abydos.

The ultimate dream is only achievable by the very wealthy and that is to be buried here, or at least have their mummies taken here before burial. If this was not possible, there was once a trend for a false burial at Abydos, meaning their *ka* was buried here in a false tomb with funerary stelae but their body was buried near their village.

Dealing with Death

Death is an inevitable part of everyone's life and the people of Kemet see death as the start of a journey into the afterlife. Here, the deceased will become *akh ikr en Re* and will live for eternity in the Fields of Reeds, one of the names the Egyptians give to the afterlife and a place that looks remarkably like the countryside in Kemet when it is in abundance.

We have discussed how ancestors are included in the household religion and how false doors in the second room of the house enable deceased family members to enter the house at will. The dead are very much a part of daily life.

So what do you do when a loved one dies? The first thing you do is obviously ensure the body is treated appropriately by sending it to the embalmers. Of course, you only need to do this if you want your loved ones to be prepared in the Egyptian way and to be mummified.

There is little need to go into the mummification details closely in a guide of this kind although it would be useful to know what you are paying for in regard to the preparation of the body. Ideally, the finished mummy should resemble a god, which will facilitate their journey into the afterlife. The body needs to be carefully preserved so that in the afterlife it can once again house the *ka* (life-force) of the deceased. This enables the deceased to use their body in the afterlife.

However, the quality of the mummification process depends on how much you are able to pay and, in general, there are two standards. The most expensive method renders the body and the internal organs fully preserved. The body is therefore considered in perfect condition for the afterlife. At the end of the process you will receive a fully wrapped mummy, which has had all the internal organs other than the heart removed and the cavities packed with sawdust and herbs. You will also receive four preserved organs, which can be placed within canopic jars in the tomb.

If you have the wealth for this level of mummification you will presumably be able to commission a set of canopic jars within which the preserved organs will be placed. Each of the four jars traditionally has a different head corresponding to a different organ and it is imperative that these are not confused:

- **Imsety** is human and protects the liver
- **Hapy** is an ape and protects the lungs
- **Duamutef**, the jackal, is responsible for the stomach
- **Qebehsenuef** is a falcon and is responsible for the intestines.

DID YOU KNOW?

The ancient Egyptians believed all thought processes and emotions happened in the heart rather than the brain. They didn't really understand the process of the brain and thought it was superfluous to requirements. Therefore, during the mummification process the brain was removed and discarded, whereas the heart was left in place.

To remove the brain the ethemoid bone at the top of the nose was broken, and the brain was removed in pieces using a hooked instrument. Experiments have shown this method was inefficient for removing the whole brain. An alternative method was used, where juniper oil and turpentine liquid were poured into the nose, dissolving the brain. This was then removed through the nostrils.

If a native of Kemet dies abroad it is considered imperative they are returned to their beloved town so they can be buried there. This is a fundamental part of the belief system and you should not be alarmed if you are greeted with 'May you die in your town'. This is not a threat of imminent death but rather a positive greeting wishing you good luck.

The funeral itself varies according to the wealth of the family. Some families will only open their family tombs once every two or three years, interring a number of bodies at the same time. If that is the case then the mummified remains will be stored in a room in their house until the funeral is to be carried out.

The funeral procession itself is an opportunity to show the community how wealthy the family is and how important the deceased person was. At the head of the funeral procession is the coffin on a sledge, followed by a second sledge bearing the canopic jars and the preserved internal organs. Then there is a procession of servants – if they have them – carrying objects to be placed in the tomb. These include beds, chairs, tables and boxes of smaller items including clothes, jewellery, food and anything else that the deceased may find useful in the afterlife.

To add to the procession, a middle-class family will hire a group of professional mourners to lament, rip their clothes and tear their hair out, all to show how well-loved the deceased was. It is considered unseemly for the widow or female members of the family to display their grief in this way so professional mourners ensure the deceased is mourned publically and at great volume (see more in the section on jobs).

In order for the mummified body to be completely functional it is essential for the Opening of the Mouth Ceremony to be carried out after the body has been wrapped. Sometimes this ritual is carried out on a statue of the deceased, although recently it has become more common to carry this out on the mummy itself. The mummy in the anthropoid coffin case is held upright at the entrance to the tomb and a priest wearing a jackal mask performs the ritual. This ceremony is carried out by a sem priest who, using an adze, ceremoniously cuts the bandages at the mouth and nose making it possible for the deceased to breathe, speak and eat in the afterlife. Then offerings of clothing, ointments, incense and food are made to the mummy.

The final aspect of the funeral is to have a final meal in the tomb chapel with the deceased and their close family and food is left on pottery plates in the chapel. This is a final opportunity for the family to spend time with the deceased until the next Beautiful Festival of the Valley.

Once the funeral is finished and the dust has settled there are regular opportunities for the family to communicate with the deceased through the giving of regular libations. This essentially means pouring water for the deceased at the tomb, thus providing them with life-giving water as well as a form of purification. Through the additional recitations of prayers and the repetition of the name of the deceased, this ensures their continued existence in the afterlife. Many tomb chapels bear an inscription asking for regular libations:

> Oh you living on earth, who will pass this tomb libate for me, for I am a master of secrets; bring me a funerary offering from your provisions, for I am one who loves men.[7]

In the newly circulated *Instructions of Ani*, which provides excellent advice on how to behave, it states:

> Libate for your father and mother who are resting in the desert valley. When the gods witness your actions, they will say 'accepted.'

There are no limits to how long it should take to make libations and it is not unheard of for people to spend three days at a time making libations for relatives who have recently become True of Voice (dead). Libations are generally only carried out for a recent death, and not necessarily for a relative who died some years previously, although of course this very much depends on the level of grief of every individual.

Staying Healthy

It is inevitable that at some point while you are in Thebes you will get ill and will need to visit the doctor or wise-woman to help bring you back to good health. As you will notice on the streets of Thebes, there are very few white-haired individuals. The average age at death in the Nile valley is nineteen years old. If individuals reach this milestone age they will live to the ripe old age of thirty for women and thirty-four for men. Naturally, this is just a guideline, and you will meet some remarkable people who have lived for fifty or sixty years. It is worth asking them what their health secrets are and trying to adopt as many of them as possible.

DID YOU KNOW?

Ancient Egyptian traditions of mummification mean this is one of the few ancient cultures where the people and their soft tissues are preserved. Egyptologists are therefore often able to identify precisely what killed the individual, what diseases they suffered from and their age at death. From this it is possible to present a clear idea of the health and age of death of this ancient community.

Bathing

The key to staying healthy is to keep as clean as possible, which is no mean feat in the climate and landscape of Kemet. Generally, rich and poor people alike wash every morning after rising and also their hands and face after eating.

The very rich may have a room in their house dedicated to ablutions. These rooms may include a toilet comprising a wooden seat resting on

Shower, palace at Medinet Habu. (Photograph by the author).

two brick pillars with a bowl of sand beneath which is then emptied outside. Some of these ablution rooms have a shower room, with a stone slab with a drain where a servant pours water over the bather.

This is beyond the reach of most people, who will simply wash themselves with water in a bowl in the home. The very poor can use the river Nile for their daily ablutions. This can also be very refreshing on a hot day. However, it is best to avoid the canals and stick to washing in the main river itself as the water in the canals do not flow and can be stagnant.

The most common soap is made from natron (a natural salt), soda and ashes. This can be a little drying on the skin so anointing with oils afterwards is necessary.

There are more than thirty scented oils available in the marketplace. These are made by mixing fragrant vegetable oils with milk, honey salts, fragrant resins and aromatic flowers such as lilies, jasmine and roses. Anointing with these is not only good for the skin but good for the nose too and they are considered so important they are included in monthly rations.

DID YOU KNOW?

Perfume is not only used on the body but also on clothes to freshen them up. In tomb scenes from the New Kingdom white linen clothes are sometimes streaked with brown. This is indicative of perfume soaked clothes.

Making Perfume

Tomb scenes from the Old Kingdom onwards show perfume making in progress. The scented parts of the plant – whether they are petals or leaves – are placed in a bowl and crushed in the same way that grapes are crushed for making wine.

These crushed plant parts are then placed in a large linen cloth with two loops at each end. A rod is put into these loops and the cloth is twisted until all of the liquid has been squeezed out of the plant pulp. This is also similar to the process of crushing grapes for wine.

This method of making perfume only uses small parts of the plant. Perfumes made this way had a shelf life of up to twenty years, especially those made with lily extract. Myrrh-based scents lasted ten years and those of cinnamon and cassia lasted a little less.

Perfume making, tomb of Iymery, Giza.

For banquets or parties it is common to wear perfume cones upon the head and these can be made at home or purchased at the market. As the evening progresses these cones melt, emanating a delightful fragrance.

Perfume cone worn by Tiy, the wife of Ay, at Amarna.

These cones are quite straightforward to make and use a technique called cold steeping. This requires placing a number of flower petals – rose or jasmine are best suited – over a layer of animal fat between two boards. These are left for a day and a night until the fat has absorbed all the fragrance. The petals are then removed and a fresh load is added. This process is repeated for a number of weeks until the fat layer is saturated with scent before it is moulded into cones.

The cones are time-consuming to produce but they are well worth it, as long as you don't skimp on the flowers. They smell wonderful as they melt but only if the smell of the flowers is more overpowering than the smell of animal fat.

Despite keeping clean however, it is quite likely that at some point you will have to visit the physician.

Visiting the Physician

Egyptian doctors are well-known throughout the world for being the best and the most effective and many of our great doctors have been sent abroad to treat foreign kings. So if you are in need of medical attention you could not be in a better place.

The best physicians are undoubtedly priests, who learn their trade at the House of Life attached to some of the greatest temples in the land. The House of Life as a great institute of learning was set up by the infamous sage Imhotep himself. He was the man responsible for designing and building the step pyramid of Djoser at Saqqara. The original House of Life was at the City of White Walls, Mennefer (Memphis), but here in Thebes we are blessed with a training centre at the temple of *ipt-swt* (Karnak).

Visiting the physicians attached to the temple of *ipt-swt* is, however, out of the price range of most people and, therefore, you will have to seek alternative care. These options vary depending on the symptoms of your illness. Generally, if an ailment is obvious, like a cut or a broken bone, a doctor is the best option as the prescribed cure will be purely medicinal, perhaps accompanied by an incantation or prayer.

If you have an ailment that is not obvious, then the cause of the problem is more likely to be of supernatural origin and it will be necessary to turn to supernatural means for a cure. For supernatural illnesses it must be considered that approaching priest physicians is not always the easiest option as it is expensive for the initial consultation, and often the cure will have an extra cost, which could be as much as constructing a new shrine for the temple.

At certain times of year the temple will be busier than others and approaching the priests may not be possible. However, if you feel the temple physicians are the only means of a cure then state your case to the doorkeeper, who can approach the priest on your behalf.

Naturally, you can also appeal directly to a deity to help you out of your predicament, but it is essential that you choose the right deity. One should approach the priests of Sekhmet, the lioness-headed deity, to aid in the cure of plagues and epidemics. She is a tricky goddess as she controls the plague, and essentially priests or sufferers will appeal to her to remove the plague which she initially caused.

With people living so closely together, diseases spread quickly and at times of need shrines to Sekhmet will be busy, so it might be worthwhile getting to know the priests while you are healthy so that you can skip the queue when there is an epidemic.

While many people wear kohl around the eyes as a means of preventing eye disease, it is still common to have eye problems. The god to approach if you are struck down with an eye disease is Duau. He is a lunar god and the patron god of ophthalmologists. There are no shrines dedicated solely to this particular deity but a priest should be able to appeal to the god on your behalf.

Bites and stings from snakes and scorpions are very common in the Nile valley and some of them can prove to be fatal if not dealt with quickly. One option is to approach the god Horus, the god of deadly stings and bites, specifically from crocodiles, snakes and scorpions. The goddess Selqet can also be approached to cure bites and stings from venomous reptiles and insects.

Village Physicians

If the temple physicians are too costly, or you consider your ailment serious enough for a doctor but not serious enough for the priests or the gods themselves, then approach the physician in your village. Often the village scribe will have knowledge of the medical papyri and may be able to administer prescriptions, or they will guide you to the local physician most suited to your particular ailment. All physicians have their own specialities such as eyes, childbirth, and stings and bites. The price for treatment will be negotiable.

Examination Procedure

When you first visit the doctor he will examine you and the procedure is likely to be similar for every doctor. He will start by asking about the problem, before conducting a physical examination which includes a study of urine, stools, sputum and blood. He will then check the pulse, 'You should put your finger on it, you should examine the belly.'[8]

The pulse is very important and can tell the doctor many things about what ails the patient because, 'It is there that every physician and every priest of Sekhmet places his fingers … he feels something from the heart.'[9]

The final test is the reflexes and the physician will 'Examine his belly and knock on his finger ... Place your hand on the patient and tap.'

Once the examination is complete the doctor will make his diagnosis. This is generally one of three decisions: 'An ailment which I will treat',

'An ailment which I will contend', or 'An ailment not to be treated'. Most doctors will try to treat every ailment but if you are told the doctor will not treat you it is recommended that you find another doctor who will.

Generally, many medicines prescribed are applied logically: medicines for invisible diseases and those likely to have a supernatural cause are taken orally; external applications are for pain; ointments for skin diseases; inhalations for respiratory diseases; gargles for mouth disorders; baths and douches for gynaecological problems and enemas for intestinal infections.

Some common ailments you will become adept at dealing with yourself without the aid of a village physician or wise-woman, and it would be advisable to learn how to produce your own remedies as it will save you time and will be cheaper in the long run. Most people self-diagnose with the literate using medical papyri as a reference, or word of mouth for the less literate. It is then possible to buy all the ingredients you need and make the medicine as required.

Bites and Stings

Bites and stings are easy to treat if the type of snake or scorpion is identified. Each creature's venom has a different treatment so knowing what bit or stung you it will help. Once the creature is identified by the doctor he will give one of three prognoses, one of which is preferable to the others: 'One does not die because of it', 'Death hastens very quickly', 'If it bites someone he will die immediately'.

The remedy will often include a 'knife treatment' to remove the venom and the wound is then packed with natron, which will hopefully reduce swelling. Additionally the doctor may prescribe 'Onion, ground finely in beer. Eat and spit out for one day.' This will help to remove the venom from your body.

Common Ailments

Indigestion can be dealt with by mixing a crushed hog's tooth into the dough of four sweet cakes. Eat these for four days, which should be enough for the indigestion to pass.

Another common ailment is diarrhoea and keeping the ingredients to hand will be better for you and your family. Locally, a tried and tested cure for diarrhoea is a mixture of figs and grapes, bread dough, pit corn, fresh earth, onion and elderberry which is to be taken internally once the diarrhoea starts and until it clears up.

Cooking on open fires, as you would expect, creates a burning hazard and should you or a family member receive a burn you should produce a compress of barley bread, animal fat and salt mixed together and bandaged over the burn. This should ease the pain and lessen the inflammation.

For a more sustained burn there is a more intense remedy and a longer list of ingredients. The specific mixture must be applied on the correct day for it to be effective.

> Day 1: black mud
> Day 2: excrement of small cattle (sheep etc.)
> Day 3: resin of acacia, barley dough, carob, oil
> Day 4: wax, oil, unwritten papyrus, *wah*-legume
> Day 5: carob, red ochre, *khes* part of *ima* tree,[10] copper flakes[11]

You can also apply some of the pain relief discussed below under the section on 'toothache'.

Unfortunately, even with the best ingredients and application according to the advice above, a burn is quite likely to get infected. You will be able to identify whether there is an infection if 'high fever/inflammation comes forth from it; its two lips are red and its mouth is open … there is great swelling.'[12] There is little you can do about it, but if you have any green pigment such as copper or malachite[13] this can be applied to the infection.

Headaches are also very common and there are numerous remedies available so it may be a case of trial and error to find one that is suitable for you. One of the most common remedies is to produce a poultice using fruit of coriander and honey. As soon as the head is bandaged the headache will dissipate.

The common cold is another nuisance that most people, young and old, suffer from at some point in their lives. Although a cold has very clear physical symptoms, there is a very important religious incantation that must be recited instead of a practical medicinal application. It may be worth learning this:

> Flow out fetid nose! Flow out son of fetid nose. Flow out, you who break the bones, destroy the skull, and make ill the seven holes.

Of course, there is no harm in producing remedies for headaches and fever in addition to this incantation just to help the symptoms to depart.

Open Wounds

The first thing a physician or wise-woman will recommend for an open wound is to clean it thoroughly with wine before it is sewn together with a needle and thread. It is always best to get someone else to do this procedure. Then it is recommended that raw meat – if available – is applied to the wound on the first day as this facilitates healing.

Application

It is important to adapt any medicament according to the age of the patient and generally 'if it is a big child, he should swallow it like a draught, if he is still in swaddles, it should be rubbed by his nurse in milk and thereafter sucked on for four days.'

It is also important to consider the time of day that a treatment is most effective. For example, for eye compresses the medical papyri state 'the eye is painted therewith in the evening its other half is dried, finely ground, and the eye is painted therewith in the morning.'

The length of time a prescription should be applied varies and there are three options: 'Until he recovers', 'until the period of his injury passes by', or 'until you know that he has reached a decision point.'[14]

Parasites

There were many common ailments which are not recorded in the medical papyri but have been identified in mummies. The Egyptians do not seem to have had treatment for these ailments. For example, most ancient Egyptians suffered from bilharzia (*schistosomiasis*), caused by the *schistsoma haematobia* worm, released by the water snail.

This miniscule worm penetrates intact skin, entering the blood stream and results in anaemia, loss of appetite, urinary infection and loss of resistance to other diseases. It was difficult to avoid this ailment as the snail lived in stagnant water found in the fields and marshes. Many people worked in these areas and stood ankle deep in this water all day, every day.

Other parasitic worms included the Guinea worm, which was contracted through drinking water infected with a small crustacean containing immature forms of the parasite that developed in the stomach. The female worm normally settles in the legs, causing ulcers, allowing eggs to be passed out of the body and back into the water supply.

Another parasite is Trichnella which was contracted by eating undercooked pork containing immature forms of the worm. These develop in the intestine and the female deposits up to 1,500 larvae which can travel into every organ of the body.

Many Egyptians would have suffered with parasitic worms but the symptoms were not diagnosed correctly and therefore not treated effectively.

Breathing Difficulties

An invisible but very debilitating infection is caused by the sand and dust which is abundant in Thebes at any time of the year. This disease is called *sand pneumoconiosis* and is often more pronounced among stone masons and tomb craftsmen who work in enclosed spaces with an excess of dust in the air.

This irritating disease causes shortness of breath and severe coughs. The only remedy that can be offered is to soothe the cough with a mixture of honey, cream, carob, and date kernels which must be heated and inhaled.

Eye Diseases

Eye diseases are tricky to self-treat for a number of reasons, including unusual ingredients and difficulty in treating your own eyes. However, it takes a strong constitution to visit an eye doctor as one of their pieces of equipment for eye ailments is a heated piece of broken glass.

It could be worth saving up ingredients in case of eye complaints and then provide the doctor with the ingredients for him to put together in the correct proportions. Many eye complaints are treated with excrement from various creatures, including lizard, crocodile, pelican and human infant.[15] Additionally blood from ox, ass, pigs, dogs and goats is also used, and, at times, human urine. When using such ingredients it is best to get advice as to the combination and application.

If the eyes are weakening and it becomes harder to see then powdered granite should be sprinkled over both eyes. This will imbue

Surgical
equipment, temple
of Kom Ombo.

the strength of the granite to penetrate into the person, providing strength, durability and beauty.

It would be necessary to go to a physician if you suffer with cataracts as the cure is a mixture of tortoise brains mixed with honey accompanied by a prayer asking gods to remove the darkness from the eye. The best god to approach regarding eye complaints or blindness is the god Ptah, although for minor eye complaints the lesser gods Duau or Mechenti-irti, the god of the blind, are appropriate for help.

Broken Bones

If you feel or hear the sickening snap of a bone all is not lost as a doctor will be able to set it. If this is done well then the limb will be usable afterwards, even if not entirely straight. Wooden splints padded with linen will be applied to broken bones and tied in place. For a bad break a cast may be applied. This is made from cow's milk, mixed with barley, or acacia leaves mixed with gum and water and remains in place until the bone has healed. With broken feet or lower limbs wearing a copper ring on the toe will aid healing and is firmly recommended.[16]

Splints

In 1908 Grafton Elliot Smith discovered two sets of splints in a cemetery at Naga ed-Deir attached to fifth dynasty (2495-2345 BCE) mummies.

One was attached to the femur of a fourteen-year-old girl and was made of wood padded with linen. The second mummy had a splint on their forearm made of acacia bark, also wrapped in linen.

Also in 1908 Frederic Wood Jones, excavating at Dakka (400 BCE to first century CE), discovered a number of bodies that had suffered from blows with a stick to the forearm and clavicle resulting in fractures. Many of the fractures had been so well set that they had healed and were barely visible.

In the Giza pyramids workman village, numerous bodies have been found with fractures to the forearm and the leg. Most of these fractures had been set and had healed completely and were also barely visible.

A common break, especially among young boys, are broken noses. These are dealt with differently to breaks of the long bones and do not really require a visit to the physician. Instructions as to what to do are quite straightforward:

> Clean out for him what is in his two nostrils with two swabs of linen, until every worm of blood, which coagulates in the interior of his nostrils, comes forth.
>
> Now, afterwards, you put two swabs of linen, moistened with oil, placed in his two nostrils. You then place for him two stiff rolls of linen, bandaged on it. You should treat him afterwards with oil and honey and lint, every day until he is well.[17]

Toothache

It's quite likely you will have toothache at one time or another and while there are plenty of doctors to choose from there are very few trained dentists. Any treatment you need you will have to administer yourself, or seek the help of the wise-woman.

Although most dental problems cannot be prevented and are just a part of everyday life in Kemet, it doesn't hurt to practice dental hygiene as a matter of course. It is advised that using a toothbrush to remove old bits of food from between the teeth can help slow down mouth infections. And the best thing is that toothbrushes are free. Simply find a twig, fray the end and use it to brush the surface of the tooth and to poke between the teeth as and when you feel you need it. After use, the surface of the teeth will feel smooth and clean.

It is also socially desirable to use breath-fresheners regularly whether you have dental problems or not. It is simply more pleasant for your colleagues and family. To clean and freshen the mouth you should chew on natron (a natural salt found in the Wadi Natron). This will be available in the marketplace for a very low price. Once the mouth has been cleansed, chewing on a cinnamon stick will freshen the breath.

Toothache is most commonly caused by extreme wear. There is little you can do to prevent this painful condition as it is caused by the food that is available throughout our beloved Kemet. For most people it is exacerbated by the cellulose and silica structures in plants and sand that is present in the flour used to form the basic ingredients of the staple food, bread. It is even said that some bakers add sand, powdered brick or stone fragments like quartz to the flour during the grinding process to speed it up.[18]

Even the rich cannot avoid this basic ingredient, unless of course you can guarantee your flour is not ground with these abrasive additions. But even a privileged diet of meat can add to this problem as collagen in meat adds to wear and tear.

So you can't prevent this from happening but you can manage the pain once you get it.

The most common side-effects of tooth wear, especially of the inner dental pulp becoming exposed, are abscesses. The majority of people in Thebes have abscesses and most have three or four at one time.[19] These are impossible to prevent, but once you have them they can be drained and the medical papyri record it as 'a disease that I treat with a knife treatment. If anything remains in pocket, it recurs.'[20]

A doctor will cut the abscess with a knife and wait for the pus to drain out and, as the papyrus explains, if anything is left inside, you will have to return for another treatment as the abscess will simply refill.

The problem with tooth abscesses is that, as people have so many of them, they ignore them and don't get them drained. This can be fatal; literally. If an abscess is left the pus will seek its own path out and will start to eat away at the bone itself. Once this happens the bone cannot be repaired and the tooth will simply fall out of the socket. In a worst case scenario the pus can make its ways to the brain, causing death.

Obviously extreme wear on the teeth and abscesses are extremely painful, and you will require some form of pain relief. Common forms of painkillers are bitter apple (colocynth), cumin, turpentine (terebinth), cow's milk, earth almonds, evening dew, chewing cloves or grinding beans with willow.[21] However, this really is a case of trial and error to see which works for you, but be aware that, depending on the individual and the condition of the teeth, some of these recommended pain killers may in fact make the infection, and the pain, worse.

It may be worth asking your friends and colleagues for advice as every family may have a different remedy that has worked for them.

A further, less common side-effect of advanced wear to the teeth is dislocation of the jaw; a painful and inconvenient affliction. For this you need to turn to a trained doctor who can pop the joint back in. A medical papyrus describes how to do this:

> When you examine a man with a lower jaw that is displaced, and you find his mouth open, so that you cannot close his mouth; then you should put your finger on the end of both jaw bones in the inside of his mouth, and put your thumbs under his chin; then you must let them (the displaced joint bone) fall together in their places ... bandage them with the *imr.w* [unknown] and honey every day until he is better.[22]

DID YOU KNOW?

The Egyptians were able to identify tooth decay although they believed it was the *fnt*-worm, or tooth worm. They believed the tunnelling of the worm caused the holes in the teeth.

Caries, or tooth decay, were in fact very rare in the dynastic period due to the low sugar diet. However, changing to a high-sugar diet during the Ptolemaic Period (post-332 BCE) saw an increase in dental caries

---

It is worth considering that such dental problems and associated pain are so common in Kemet as to be considered normal. Therefore you will not get any days off work because of it. Everyone is expected to manage the pain effectively and get on with life.

The Village Wise-Woman

While male physicians will treat both men and women, the village wise-woman will specialise in feminine health, in addition to remedies for other day-to-day conditions.

Most villages will have at least one wise-woman and a group of young women she is training so when you move into your new home make it your business to find out who the wise-woman is and what her speciality is. As these medical skills are passed down for generations it is a good idea to identify the lineage as well, to ensure the wise-woman comes from a long line of wise-women. This will guarantee that the treatment you get is tried and tested.

Conceiving a Child

Once you have settled into your new home you may consider starting a family, and this would be the honourable and right thing to do. It is important to have many children, especially boys, so that in old age you will be looked after. A man is respected and admired on account of his progeny and he is happy if his children are many, but unfortunately it seems there are many people who find this simple natural act of reproduction impossible.

There are two very simple and practical responses to this problem. The easiest is divorce, as through a different choice of spouse both the man and the woman may have a better chance of conceiving. However, if divorce is not the right option for you it would be worth visiting the wise-woman to see if she can help with conception.

First of all, it is best to test whether the infertility lies within the woman, as is often the case. It is almost impossible to tell if a man is infertile, although the husband may be *Shw* (empty). All you have to do to prove this is to look at a couple who have remarried. Sometimes with a different husband an apparently barren woman conceives within months, sometimes even weeks, although her first husband remains childless even in a second or third marriage. It does not take the genius of Thoth to work out that men can be infertile too.

The secret to a woman's fertility is a smooth run from her vagina to all other parts of her body, and it is easy to test that all the channels are open with no blockages. This test can be conducted in two ways. One is to mix beer and dates together in a bowl and the woman must sit over it. If she feels the urge to vomit then all her tubes are open and she will conceive. If you count the number of times she vomits that tells you the number of times she will conceive. Despite the unpleasantness of multiple evacuations, every woman who takes the test is begging all the gods in the pantheon that she will vomit. If there is no response then she won't conceive.

An alternative is to mix the seeds of a crushed plant – available from the wise-woman – with the milk of the mother of a new son. Then the woman desiring pregnancy should drink this mixture. If she vomits she will become pregnant but if she passes wind she won't.

Inducing vomiting is not suitable for all women. If this is the case the onion test does an equally good job of identifying fertility. The onion is inserted into the woman's vagina at night and in the morning, if her breath smells of onion, then the channels from her vagina to the rest of her body are open and she will conceive.

This is a test you can carry out yourself at home without the embarrassment of visiting a wise-woman or a doctor, as is the tell-tale examination of the veins on the breasts. Examine the breasts first thing in the morning, after rubbing fresh oil into them. If the veins on the breasts appear fresh and normal then the woman is likely to bear children, whereas if the veins are green and dark, she may bear children, albeit a little later in life. So be patient.

If the veins are broken and sunken then it is in the hands of the gods whether you will conceive. If this is the case then appeal to Hathor, as she is the only one who can grant you your wish of a child.

Adoption

In this situation adoption may be the answer. Sadly, in our world there are many orphans whose parents have died of disease, accidents or old age. As a childless couple you may choose to take one of these innocent children who has not yet developed faults into your lives and your home.

Adoption is quite simple; the chosen child simply moves in with the childless couple and they start referring to each other as mother, father, son or daughter. No official documentation or ceremony is needed, although such an important occasion cannot pass without a celebration and there is likely to be an occasion to mark this in the village.

As there are no restrictions on who can adopt there are also no limits to the age of the adopted 'child'. If you are an older couple you could choose to adopt an adult. This solves the problem of care in old age, as well as the legacy, which normally passes onto one's children, but without the stress of looking after a young child. An adopted son holds the same position in society as a natural 'eldest son', allowing the new parents to choose who their 'eldest son' is to be.

Many couples, however, feel that adoption is not right for them and prefer to have their own child. Many turn to the gods, leaving offerings to the cow-headed goddess Hathor in particular, or sleeping at the sanatorium and hoping to receive a message from 'The Golden' in a dream, which may guide them onto the correct path to conception.

Contraceptive

Some women, however, are at the opposite end of the scale and will do anything to prevent a pregnancy. Perhaps they have got many children and cannot deal physically or economically with another baby, or perhaps they are prostitutes or dancers and a child may hinder them in trying to make a living. For others, a further pregnancy is a health hazard and could endanger the mother's life.

Whatever the reason a woman does not wish to conceive, there are methods which can prevent this from happening. This is one of the very few situations where praying to the gods will not help, for while there are many deities who will help with conception, there are none who prevent pregnancy.

The most effective and easiest method for preventing a second pregnancy is to continue breastfeeding the first child for as long as possible. Generally, most babies suckle for up to three years as this provides the cleanest, healthiest and safest food for them. However, nursing can help to carefully plan when the next pregnancy occurs. This method, while being safe for the woman, is not always effective, and it is still possible to fall pregnant while breastfeeding.

Additionally, on a social level this does not work for the upper-middle classes, who often hire wet nurses to suckle their children. It would be inappropriate for a woman in this situation to suggest the wet nurse be released from her position so the mother can feed the child herself. This would, potentially, be social suicide for her. In this situation, it perhaps would be more appropriate to turn to other methods of contraception.

The most popular of which is the absorbent pad which is simply placed within the vagina. It soaks up the semen, thus preventing pregnancy. The most effective material from which to make this pad is dried crocodile dung mixed with honey. Although the collecting of the dung is dangerous, it is surprisingly odour free once it has been dried and the honey makes a more malleable texture so that the finished product can mould itself to your body shape.

This contraceptive is very effective, and invaluable if you don't want to get pregnant. The frequency of your marital activity obviously dictates how often you need to replace this 'pad', although you will probably be surprised how little marital activity there is once your husband finds out your method of contraceptive!

If this contraceptive does not appeal to you, then an alternative is to use a mixture of acacia, carob and dates, ground to as fine a powder as you can possibly get and then mixed with honey. Coat a piece of linen with this mixture and place it within the vagina. This is effective enough to prevent pregnancy for as long as you use it.

Pregnancy Tests

Obviously, when you want to become pregnant you stop using contraceptive and, if you are fertile, then you should become pregnant relatively quickly. The most obvious indication of pregnancy, assuming the woman is healthy, is the halting of the monthly cycle. Then, in order to check this is a sign of pregnancy, the onion test (discussed above) can be reapplied.

This time, if the channels are blocked by a baby the onion will not reach the breath by morning. If there is no baby then the onion's odour will be on the breath. Depending on whether pregnancy is welcome or not affects the reaction to the smell or absence of it.

There are, however, more practical and oftentimes more reliable ways to check for pregnancy. There are simple observations you can make at home, such as checking for a quickened pulse on the wrist or neck. If you are pale and unhealthy looking, or if you are feeling nauseous or suffering bouts of vomiting, there is a distinct possibility that there is a baby on the way. Also any changes to your behaviour can also be a good indication of pregnancy; do once-favoured perfumes or favourite foods now cause nausea and vomiting? Are you desiring strange food that you don't normally eat?

Once a woman is pregnant it is advisable to start worshipping the goddess Taweret, the hippopotamus goddesses (discussed above). The pregnant woman should either wear an amulet of the goddess or get a small statue to place in the household shrine and make offerings on a daily basis.

Removing a Pregnancy

If a pregnancy is not welcome there is a remedy which will cause whatever is in your womb to be given to the earth, but you should be very clear that this is what you want, as the effects cannot be reversed. This is too dangerous to be done at home and should be carried out under the supervision of the village wise-woman or the midwife. Sometimes they are the same person, but I wouldn't recommend going to the doctor. You need a woman's touch for this.

The remedy is simply to sit upon a mixture made from the *niaia* plant, although its preparation has to be carefully carried out, and should not be attempted yourself.

Identification of the Sex of the Baby

A woman happy in her fertility will start pondering on whether the child is a girl or a boy. While both are acceptable in modern society, many couples prefer to have a boy, especially for their first child. It is important for every couple to have at least one son to follow in the footsteps of their father by taking over his career when the time comes. Sons are also particularly useful in old age, as any daughters will be married, running their own households and caring for their in-laws. The duty of the eldest son in particular is to care for his aging parents. His wife may even be living in his parents' home so that it is easier for him to do his duty and uphold the laws of *Maat*.

The test to find out if the child is male or female is relatively simple and can be carried out at home without the aid of a doctor or wise-woman. The woman requires two small cloth packets with a small amount of soil in each. One packet should contain emmer wheat seeds and the other barley seeds. The woman must urinate over both packets every day.

It is important to keep monitoring the seeds as the test is based on which sprouts first. If the wheat sprouts first then a boy will be born; if the barley sprouts first it will be a girl. However, if neither sprouts then there is no baby and the couple must continue trying. This news often brings great sadness.

Keeping Safe During Pregnancy

Once pregnancy has been determined it is important for the expectant mother to keep safe as it is a very dangerous time. Every woman's fear during pregnancy is that she will see a flow of blood as this often indicates the child has died in the womb and the pregnancy is at an end.

There isn't much that can be done to prevent a miscarriage. Most women are unable to stay in bed during their pregnancy because they have to care for their other children, look after the home or even work in the fields. Full bed-rest is really the only way of keeping safe at this time, but this is impractical for all but the wealthiest women.

All pregnant women turn to the gods for help and any god can aid in protecting an expectant mother if the prayers are said with conviction. However, as discussed in the chapter on beliefs, Hathor, Taweret and Bes are the most popular deities for expectant mothers.

Alternatively there is a popular prayer to be recited to the jackal-headed god Anubis in his form as Opener of the Ways. This prevents miscarriage from happening using the inundation – which is a time of great fertility – as a metaphor for the blood that indicates the child has Gone Forth by Day (died):

> Anubis has come forth to keep the inundation from treading on what is pure ... This spell is to be said over threads of the border of *yaat* fabric with a knot made in it. To be applied to the inside of the vagina.

Whilst the prayer is very important, one mustn't forget the knotted *yaat* fabric, which is placed within the body. This is the magical element of the prayer, as the prayer prevents the fabric from being soiled by blood, and the fabric itself enables the expectant mother to monitor the situation.

All expectant mothers are concerned throughout their pregnancy for the safety of their child, be they peasant farmers or royalty, and this concern increases as the term nears completion, a most dangerous time for both the child and the mother. To make the process safer, it is essential to employ the services of a good midwife. Most villages have one. Even if she is not medically trained, the experience she has gained birthing the villages' children will be enough. She should, however, know the incantations and rituals that are required as well as practical things such as when to push and how to safely cut the umbilical cord. She should also be aware of the correct way to prepare your hair for the birth. Although you may be wondering why on earth you would be worrying about your hair at a time like this, it is, in fact, an important part of sympathetic magic associated with the birth. Your hair should be bound as tightly as you can stand it, tied in little locks, which are slowly loosened at the appropriate moment during labour and helping to release the baby at the best time. Your hair cannot be too loose otherwise the baby could come too soon and be in danger.

There are also medical practices to help the child to be born easily and safely. These should only really be used if the child is refusing to be released from the mother's womb. If the baby has exceeded its term then a complicated mixture, best obtained from your local wise-woman, of incense resin, *besbes* plant, juniper berries, *ished* fruit, resin from a fir tree, an onion, Lower Egyptian salt and the *niaia* plant, mixed with beer and fly excrement can be used to encourage the birth. This mixture is moulded into a ball or a lozenge and inserted into the vagina. As this mixture contains *niaia* plant it is best not to try to make it at home as this plant, used in the wrong quantities, can cause all that is in the womb to flow into the earth. Used in the correct proportions it can hasten the birth.

The gentlest form of encouragement for the baby, which should be used if the labour pains have been going on a little too long, comprises a bandage applied to the stomach. This bandage should

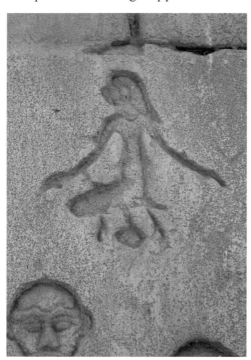

be coated in a mixture of salt from Lower Egypt, white emmer, incense resin, the *sut hemet* plant, a small part of a tortoise, *hekun* beetle, beer and pine oil, mixed into a paste using oil and fat. The essence of this mixture soaks through the stomach, encouraging the child to leave the womb.

The best position for a woman in labour is squatting on the floor, and if possible a birthing brick should be placed under each foot. These should be decorated with images of Bes, Taweret, Heqat and Meskenet, all important deities for childbirth, and will protect the mother during labour.

Hieroglyph showing childbirth, Edfu.

A bowl of hot water infused with aromatic herbs is placed between the woman's feet. The steam will open up the channels between the vagina and the womb and make the baby's descent easier. Throughout labour the midwife will recite prayers and incantations invoking various deities to help in repelling the demons who wish to cause harm. It is essential that she is not interrupted during these incantations as each one needs to be recited perfectly to be effective.

One particularly important prayer is to the god Bes, which should be recited over a clay statue of the god at the head of the pregnant woman. To avoid the risk of the amulet falling to the floor you could create a headdress with a Bes amulet placed at the forehead. This prayer is recited loud and clear by the midwife:

> Come down, placenta, come down, come down! I am Horus who conjures in order that she who is giving birth becomes better than she was, as if she was already delivered ... Look, Hathor will lay her hand on her with an amulet of health! I am Horus who saves her!

Although the midwife is supposed to recite the prayer, there is no harm in memorising it yourself, whether you are the pregnant woman or an observer and helper on the day. Just remember to recite it four times if you want it to be effective.

These prayers are further facilitated by ensuring an ivory birthing wand, decorated with images of protective deities, touches the pregnant woman's stomach and vagina until the birth is complete. When the baby is born the wand should be placed on the baby to ensure any demons attached to it will enter the wand and leave the baby in safety. The midwife may do this herself, or she may allocate the task to one of the women in attendance. It is an important job so listen to the midwife's instructions and follow them to the letter.

Once the baby is born the midwife will attend to it, listening carefully to the first sound it makes, which predicts the health of the child. If the fist cry is *ny*, the child will live, but if the sound is *mebi* the child will die.

The umbilical cord is then cut using a ceremonial knife called a *peshef kaf*, which has been used for this procedure for thousands of years. If the individual family cannot afford their own ritual instruments for every birth, the midwife can bring her own, and models can be provided by the family for ritualistic purposes.

The final trauma for the new mother is the delivery of the *ka* of the child, or the placenta. The midwife will treat this almost like the birth of another infant. This is taken away with the umbilical cord and preserved, sometimes even mummified, and remains with the baby all its life. It is also placed in the tomb of the child, no matter how many decades later he or she may need it. The new mother is now free to rest, and her attendants should make her comfortable on a bed or mat while the baby is washed, before being brought to her.

The last role of the midwife is to prepare soothing remedies for the new mother. One remedy is designed to help shrink the uterus back to normal proportions after the birth and is made using the *kheper-wer* plant, carob, milk and honey, strained and placed in the vagina. It has a soothing effect and may ease the discomfort of birth a little. Whilst the midwife does not charge (or should not charge) for her services – although there are some very unscrupulous women out there – it is always a nice idea to offer her a gift, perhaps of good quality linen or even a chicken or goat, and also to have the ingredients ready for the remedies needed during childbirth and the aftercare. Though the midwife will provide the ingredients if necessary, she will have paid for these herself and therefore is a cost incurred by her. If she uses your ingredients, it is like an extra payment for her and she will be grateful for it.

Confinement

After birth some women believe that confinement is the only way of remaining healthy and safe. How this is carried out varies from home to home, depending on availability and desire. Some families are lucky enough to have a confinement chamber beneath the stairs, known as a *hrryt*. Some mothers even give birth in this chamber.

Although these spaces are small they should be beautifully decorated with images of the god Bes, as a symbol of protection, or elaborate images of convolvulus leaves, which are both romantic and erotic and emphasise that this is a place for fertile women. The new mother should remain in here for fourteen to twenty days to really ensure her and the child's safety. This of course is not practical for every woman.

Some women have too many commitments in the home to take up to twenty days out. Unless you have servants, this is not always practical. Those who are unable to practice confinement should try to rest as much as possible and try not to do any work that would put them in danger; so no working in the fields or down by the river. However, if you have to work, do not worry; worship the gods and increase your daily ritual worship of Bes, Taweret and the ancestors and you should be safe.

On day seven after the child is born there is the naming ceremony. This entails all the women in the village descending on your house and talking to you through the curtain to the *hyyt*. Names are important in Kemet. They are not only a means of identification but also an element of the personality of the individual. A name is therefore chosen very carefully. It can be one that will protect the child throughout their life, one that expresses affiliation with a god or king or one that would describe the type of person the child will grow up to be.

Before the ceremony it is essential that both the new mother and child are purified, which means a long luxurious wash or shower, should you have the facilities, with lovely scented oils to make mother and baby smell and feel refreshed. It is a great day and should be a time of great celebration for the entire village.

Depression

Sometimes after childbirth a mother may feel melancholy, although this is, of course, not restricted to new mothers. Anyone can suffer from what is commonly known as 'Fever in the heart', 'Dryness of the heart', 'Falling of the heart' or 'Kneeling of the mind'. Some doctors feel it is an ailment that is attributed frequently to women and is described as 'A woman who loves bed, she does not rise, and does not shake it'.[23] This is due to a wandering uterus and the cure is to drink two *henu* of a mixture called *khaui* and then encourage her to vomit the mixture back out.

A remedy for depression, as well as any other ailment of the mind or body, is temple sleep and this is something wholly recommended if your budget can stretch to it. Through entering the temple sanatorium and falling asleep, aided by the warmth, the incense and the incantations of the priests, the mind can be opened to receiving messages from the gods themselves. The priests are able to interpret your dreams, which are the conduit through which the god speaks to you, and how they suggest the depression, illness or worry can be addressed. While in the temple water dripped over statues inscribed with prayers designed to heal is provided so those who are ill can drink it, or wash in it.

Often a cure or peace of mind will be granted by the god if a donation is made to the temple. This could be a meat offering for something small, or commissioning and constructing a new shrine for something more challenging.

Dream Interpretation

Kenhirkhepshef, a scribe during the reign of Ramses II at Deir Medina, wrote a list of dream interpretations. The papyrus is known as the Chester Beatty III papyrus and the dream interpretations are on the rear.

It is possible that the villagers approached Kenhirkhepshef with their dreams and asked him for guidance. If this is the case it provides an insight into the worries and concerns of the villagers.

The dreams are varied in their subject matter with seeing objects such as the moon, a prison, a wagon, wildlife such as cranes, lotus flowers, or animals being common. There was also a preoccupation with food provision, prestige, and personal wealth, as well as divine concerns. Dreams about sex only featured in four per cent of the dreams.

One fifth of all dreams recorded were about the giving and receiving of gifts, which was an essential part of the village economy.

The dreams and interpretations were laid out in a table format thus:

If a man sees himself in a dream... Dead ... Good: it means long life in front of him

If a man sees himself in a dream ... Uncovering his own backside ... Bad: he will be an orphan later

If a man sees himself in a dream ... Writing ... Bad: reckoning up of his misdeeds by his god.

The interpretations were based around language more than anything, with the use of rhyming couplets and linguistic puns, or the dream and the meaning were reversed, such as death meaning long life.

Stepping Out in Style

Thebes is the capital city of Kemet and therefore is the centre of culture, fashion and arts. Consequently, if you are to blend in while in Thebes you will need to look the part. As discussed in the chapter of health, keeping clean and smelling fresh is essential and should be a first consideration. In addition to this, both men and women are conscientious about hair removal.

Hair Removal

On the whole, men are clean-shaven so it is best to invest in a sharp razor and a whetstone or find a barber you trust. Barbers generally travel between villages shaving and cutting hair so this is something you can investigate when you have settled in. The *Instruction of Dua-Khety* describes the role:

> The barber labours until dusk. He travels to a town, he sets
> himself up in his corner, And moves from street to street for
> a customer.

Having facial hair will make a newcomer stand out in Thebes as a 'barbarian'; essentially someone who is not Egyptian. The only Egyptians who have facial hair are in mourning as during the period of grief personal adornment becomes secondary and men are expected to grow a beard.

A very popular love poem comparing the feeling of love to grief describes all the things that are abandoned:

> When I think of my love of you,
> It makes me act not sensibly,
> It leaps from its place.

It lets me not to put on a dress,
Nor wrap my scarf around me:
I put no paint upon my eyes,
I'm not even anointed.

Women in general in Kemet have very smooth, anointed skin and spend a great deal of time removing body hair with a combination of copper razors or tweezers. Oil is used as a lubricant to ensure a smooth shave and prevent a rash from forming.

If razors are not convenient then hair removal cream is available and is made from the boiled and crushed bones of birds mixed with fly dung, oil, sycamore juice, gum and cucumber. It is heated up and placed on the skin then ripped off when cooled, removing the hair beneath.

Eyebrows tend to be heavy in Kemet and not plucked to thin lines as one sees in other cultures. The thicker and longer the eyebrows the better as this will then require less cosmetics to get the desired fashion of brows reaching the hairline (see section on cosmetics below).

Wigs

Hair is essential to any Theban-ready outfit, but what newcomers may find strange is that most Egyptians – both men and women – often shave their heads and wear a wig instead. This practice is partially for reasons of fashion and partially for health, as in the hot weather hair can harbour all manner of lice and fleas and, therefore, cleanliness is easier to maintain with a shaved head.

Erotic Hair

Hair in ancient Egypt was considered very erotic and the mention of women dressing their hair or donning wigs is made in literature and love poetry almost as if they were in a state of undress.

In the *Tale of the Two Brothers* (1199-1193 BCE) the younger brother interrupts his sister-in-law as she is braiding her hair, which was seen as erotic. She propositions him but he refuses due to being a loyal brother. However, she reports to her husband that his brother had, in fact, propositioned her, saying, 'Come, let us spend an hour lying together: loosen your braids'. This line has also been translated as 'don your wig' and both illustrate the close association with hair and sex.

The act of braiding one's hair is also mentioned in a New Kingdom love poem (Papyrus Harris 500):

> My heart thought of my love for you, when half of my hair was braided;
>
> I came at a run to find you, and neglected my hairdo.
>
> Now if you let me braid my hair, I shall be ready in a moment.

Hair was also used as a sexual tool by dancers and acrobats. They wore long wigs with weights plaited into the bottom, which gave the hair a magnificent swinging motion focusing the attention of those watching.

Obviously the quality of the wig varies depending on budget and can be made of human hair, horse hair, sheep's wool or even plant fibres. The cheapest wigs are made of red palm fibre and look completely unrealistic, but you are likely to see many of these amongst the poorer classes of Theban society.

The best quality wigs are made of human hair and should consist of as many as 120,000 hairs woven into the mesh skull cap. If it seems thin make sure the price reflects this. Also ensure the hair is glued into place with bee's wax and resin. If not it will fall out when it's worn and cleaned. The very rich will wear a high-quality wig but ensure it is placed on the head in such a manner that the natural hairline is clearly seen, thus showing they are wealthy enough to maintain clean and healthy hair and therefore do not need to shave it off.

At the moment in Thebes it is fashionable to have full wigs which brush the shoulders, if not longer. The most fashionable is known as a tri-partite wig, where the very heavy hair is separated into three sections, one to fall over each shoulder to the front and a thicker section to the back. These can be embellished with complicated curls and plaits to make them fuller and more interesting. The more complicated the style and design the more difficult the wig is to clean and maintain; this, therefore, shows wealth as staff will be employed to carry out the task. Women will further embellish their wig with a decorative headband placed around the forehead and tied at the back. These can be flowers – lotus flowers are popular – a tapestry or embroidered band.

For people who maintain their natural hair – but which is thin or thinning – instead of a full wig, hair pieces are often used. These can also be used to add extra volume to a wig for that special occasion.

Dyed Wigs

The majority of wigs were black in ancient Egypt, except the cheap ones made of palm fibres, which had a reddish hue. However, it was not unheard of for the king to wear a wig dyed blue or green.

In the Old Kingdom tomb of Merysankh III (2558-2532 BCE), the wife of Khafre, the queen, is depicted in a short wig, which had been dyed red and yellow.

More common, however, was the use of henna to dye the hair. This has been attested from mummified remains, which also show henna stains to the hands and nails. One elderly lady, for example, was buried with distinctive white roots, indicating she did not have time to redo them before she died.

Wearing wigs can be hot and can make your head sweat. Coupled with the oil and grease from perfume oils and perfume cones (see above), wigs will need regular cleaning to keep them looking their best. Of course, you can clean them yourself, or you can take them to the wig workshop for a professional job.

A very good workshop is situated on the west bank, near the temple of Djeser Djeseru (Deir el Bahri). Not only do they make wigs there but they also repair and clean them.

DID YOU KNOW?

Excavations of this workshop have revealed lots of information about wig manufacture and maintenance.

Remnants of a waxy soap made from natron and soda was discovered. This was likely to have been used for the washing of wigs and hair.

A further dark brown substance of bicarbonate of manganese and quartz grains was also discovered, which would have given the natural-hair wigs body and shine. If mixed with a waxy substance it could also have been used for a hair dye.

Cosmetics

Men, women, kings, queens and gods in Kemet wear cosmetics every day, regardless of wealth, status and occupation. This is something you will have to get used to if you want to fit in to your newly adopted city. Although cosmetics are an enhancement on appearance they also have a medicinal purpose as eye make-up is worn to prevent eye infections. Kohl around the eyes can reflect the hot desert sun and repel flies, which you will soon discover are persistent.[24] A doctor can show you how to apply it in the most effective way.

Eye make-up is applied using kohl sticks, more commonly known as 'pleasure wood', though they can be made of various materials such as hematite, glass or bronze. They are thickened and flattened at one end

Doctor applying cosmetics in the tomb of Ipuy, Valley of the Nobles. (Drawing after Nunn, 1996, fig 3.6).

and are used both to mix the substance and to apply it to the eyes. It is probably best to get a personal 'pleasure wood' rather than share one with other members of your family.

The eye make-up itself comes in mineral form ground into a fine powder. This should be stored in a kohl pot and mixed with water and resin when it is required. Only mix what you will need to use as, once mixed, it does not stay fresh and dries out very quickly. The simplest way of applying kohl around the eye is to take a drop of the freshly mixed cosmetic and drop it into the corner of the eye. Tears will then help to spread it evenly along the lash line. To maintain a fashionable look, green is applied to the brows and the corner of the eyes and grey galena to the rims and lashes. Then a darker line is drawn from the corner of the eye to the hairline and the eyebrow is extended likewise.

So, what are the best cosmetics made of? Green eye-makeup is made from malachite and dark-grey is made of galena, which is imported from the Sinai Peninsula and the Eastern Desert, and the price reflects this. There is nothing more exciting at the marketplace than when the traders with the eye-paint are in town selling their wares. The queues of men and women waiting to buy the freshly imported eye-paint can be very long. In fact, these events are considered so special that many people even depict traders with eye-paint in their tombs ensuring they will have an endless supply for eternity.

Eye-paint also has religious associations and is associated by some with the god Osiris – hence its inclusion in tombs – with black eye-paint representing the fertility of the Nile silt and green representing freshness and fertility of new plants. In a funerary context, black eye-paint was offered to the left eye of the deceased – associated with the day and the sun – while green eye-paint is offered to the right eye, which is associated with the night and the moon. Adorning the deceased with eye-paint in this way helps with their divine journey into the afterlife.

However, cosmetics are also an essential aspect of day-to-day life and the adornment of the living too. If you can't afford to pay extra for imported minerals it is still perfectly acceptable to wear just black eye-paint which is easily produced at home from sunflower soot, charred almond shells and frankincense.

Eye make-up is the bare minimum that the average Thebanite wears on a daily basis but some women go further, adding rouge and lipstick to their final look. Both are made from haematite and red ochre mixed with vegetable oil or animal fat until it can be spread upon the cheeks or lips.[25] This is a new trend in cosmetics which is gaining in popularity and some say even the queen herself wears rouge.

To remove cosmetics at the end of the day use a cleanser consisting of sediments of fat mixed with lime or chalk followed by an application of perfumed oil to soothe the skin.

What to Wear

For the most part choosing what to wear is not difficult, as there are really only two styles of garment available for both men and women; the long tunic or the short tunic combined with a kilt.

When choosing your basic tunic – long or short – you should buy the best quality linen you can afford. Don't be afraid of buying used linen either. It is always possible to reuse fine-quality linen and disguise worn patches. Good quality linen is identified by how fine it is. If it is transparent by design, and not by wear then it is a good quality. If you don't want transparent, although it is the height of fashion at the moment, then you can tell the quality by how it drapes. Hold up a few cubits by one corner, if it falls in lovely pleats and folds that move in the wind, start your negotiations, but if it hangs in stiff, unmoving folds then move onto the next market stall. You want your clothes to hang on your body in a natural way with fabric that moves with your body, not against it.

The colour of the linen will be dependent on the age of the flax when it was stripped for the fibres and is not a reflection of quality. You are, therefore, able to choose shades from white to golden brown and this means you can match the linen to your skin-tone to ensure you always look at the peak of health.

While your tunic may hang beautifully when you are naked, once you have put your loin cloth on, if it is the wrong fit then it will show through the tunic and make your hips look bulky. Loincloths are simple to make and, if possible, you should have enough to wear a clean one every day, though many people in Thebes only own one or two at the most.

Loincloths are triangular in shape with two corners being long enough to tie around the waist. The third point of the triangle will be pulled through the legs and pulled over the knot at the waist. To get the best fit, the top edge of the loincloth should be inverted rather than straight so that the overall garment is arrow-head shaped. This ensures there is no excess fabric around the back of the waist. The ties at the front should also not be too long otherwise there will be a bulky knot and excess fabric hanging loose. If buying ready-made loincloths remember they should come with a short sash as well to help hold them in place.

DID YOU KNOW?

In Tutankhamun's tomb more than 145 loincloths were found but only ten tunics. It is thought that robbers had taken the tunics as an easily saleable commodity.

Kilts are very easy to wear and are made of six or more cubits of rectangular shaped linen. The corner on the short end is held against the belly button and the fabric is then wrapped around the waist two and a half times. Whatever fabric remains is scrunched together in one hand and tucked into the waistband. The front of the kilt is therefore shorter than the back and this should be taken into consideration when you are planning the length. The longer the initial fabric the bigger the bundle is that is tucked into the front of the kilt. For men it is very fashionable to have maybe two or three cubits of spare fabric here, to show wealth. In order to prevent the kilt from coming unravelled a sash is tied over the waistband to one side. The ends of the sash should not hang lower than the hem of the kilt. To accompany the kilt, you will need a tunic which reaches to the waist.

Accessories to Tunics

Tunics can either be plain linen or they can have pleats across the chest. The pleats should be created before the chest panel is stitched to the skirt. Getting sharp pleats that will withstand wear and washing is not easy, and it may be best to go to a professional dressmaker.

Tunics can also be accessorised by adding bright, decorative collars or new sleeves. Most tunics come with standard long sleeves reaching to the wrist and made of the same linen as the tunic. These are easy to

A nineteenth
dynasty statue
in the Imhotep
Museum,
Saqqara.

remove: you can either leave them off entirely, creating a perfect summer tunic and leaving your arms open to the rays of Ra, or you can add a different set of sleeves. If your tunic has a pleated section over the chest then why not have plain sleeves as a contrast, or pleated sleeves going in the opposite direction.

Alternatively, you can add a collar and these are widely available from any able seamstress. Imported tapestry collars are beautiful and come from either Syria or Nubia and are both colourful and patterned, making any plain, white tunic something worthy of royalty. Even if you have a brightly coloured and patterned collar, you can further embellish it with beads, rosettes and sequins if you have them.

Coloured sashes are also an interesting way to brighten up a plain tunic. Sashes can be made of coloured wool, tapestry, or coloured linen, with a fringed or a plain edge. When tying them around the waist both ends should reach the bottom of your tunic while being wrapped twice around the waist.

A shawl is another vital accessory to the Theban wardrobe, preferably with a fringe, which can be used on a winter evening to keep you warm, or it can be built into your overall outfit to give you fuller sleeves. Simply throw the shawl, either triangular or rectangular, over your shoulders and your tunic and cross the two ends over your chest. Then tightly tie a sash around your waist over the top of the shawl at the front and the back. If the shawl is big enough your arms will be covered and will make your top half look bigger, giving the appearance of cubits and cubits of linen where in fact only a few cubits are used.

For cold winter evenings you will need a full-length cloak, which can either be made from heavy, thick linen, which reaches the ankles and is wide enough to join at the front. As this won't be washed as often as a tunic you can dye this a deep blue or red colour.

Headdresses

For the summer, it is necessary to protect the head from the harsh rays of Ra and the most common headdress is the kerchief which is generally made of good quality linen. Everyone from farmers to royalty wears these on a daily basis.

They vary in price, depending on the length of fabric used, and can cost as much as twenty-five *deben*, five times the price of a cheap tunic. A better and more stylish headscarf is the *khat*, which is a semi-circular piece of material with the curved end left hanging over the neck and held in place with a headband. Whilst the headscarf should always be undyed linen to counter the heat, the headband can always be decorated with flowers or patterns, or simply made of coloured linen.

Jewellery

No outfit – for both men and women – is complete without a necklace, bracelet or earrings. Of course, what you choose to wear in regard to colour, material and size is dependent on personal taste.

While Thebes is resplendent with jewellery makers it is best to shop around and go to different craftsmen for different types of jewellery. For example, for faience jewellery, essential for everyday wear, you should go to a small craftsman working out of his home, as his wares will be crafted with care. If you go to the larger workshops for faience all of their beads are mould-made and you are more than likely to bump into someone wearing the same necklace. A small craftsman does not have such luxuries as clay moulds, and while you may have to wait longer for your finished item, you can guarantee that it will be unique.

In the case of gold or silver jewellery, should you be wealthy enough to buy silver, you should go to one of the temple workshops, or the most expensive craftsmen you can afford. The reason for this should be obvious. The temple workshops have the pick of the best materials as they make jewellery not only for public purchase but also for the temple itself and even the king. They will only ever use the best materials, so even if you are only going to own one gold or silver item of jewellery in your life you should ensure it is the best.

When choosing silver or gold you should be aware of their religious connotations. Silver is associated with the moon and, therefore, if you are a devotee of lunar deities such as Khonsu (the decider of a lifespan), or Thoth (the god of scribes and intelligence), then silver is the correct metal for you. The bones of the gods are silver and are strong and durable; if this reflects your personality then this is for you. However, if you are primarily a solar worshipper then gold is the ideal metal as it is everlasting and radiates like the sun.

At a temple workshop you will have the choice of buying mould-made beads, which you can ask to be strung together in a collar in the order you choose, or you can get bespoke jewellery made. This is not cheap but will be well worth the effort, even for the look of envy on the faces of your friends when you wear it.

Other items that are guaranteed to make you stand out from the crowd can be obtained from the stonemasons. Granite beads make a stunning necklace, or semi-precious stones such as amethyst, garnet, feldspar, jasper, cornelian or lapis lazuli. Carving beads from stone is not a simple task and you need specialist equipment to do so. The best stone bead-makers can be found in Deir el Medina, as most of the men work with stone every day. Some of the stone work is so intricate you would assume it had been created by Ptah himself.

For situations where a cumbersome collar is not appropriate you can simply wear a row of beads, either one or three cubits long so it hangs over your chest. For days when you are feeling a little under the weather you can incorporate an amulet into your row of beads. Should you be pregnant, a Bes or Taweret amulet should be worn, and new mothers should wear an amulet of a crescent moon in order to protect the flow of milk.

Less attractive, but very important for new mothers who are breastfeeding, is the necklace of magic knots which acts as protection against demons who would make the breasts sore and dry up. While the number of knots is not specified, seven would be ideal as this is a sacred and magical number.

Armlets, as the name would suggest, go around the tops of your arms and are tight fitting whereas bracelets go around the wrist and are looser. Armlets should be at least three fingers wide if they are to be striking, and ideally in a solid material like gold or silver, but this is not within everyone's financial reach. Instead, you could go for copper, which is cheaper, or even a decorated leather. There are some very skilled leather workers around who can carve patterns and pictures onto the leather and buff it so it shines like polished ebony. If you can get four made you will have a set of armlets and anklets that match.

If you like semi-precious stones but do not have the budget then the relatively new introduction of glass is the answer. It is made from sand in a similar way to faience but is moulded while hot whereas faience is more like clay. And while almost anyone can make faience, it is not possible to make glass in the home unless you have a furnace, so you will have to go to a professional glass-maker. Although it is fragile, glass jewellery is certainly striking as the colour is actually within the jewellery, not on the outside as with faience. Glass is the closest replica to semi-precious stones and unless you look very closely you cannot tell the difference. Rounded earplugs and ear buttons are particularly common in glass and are so beautiful when glimpsed beneath a wig.

Shoes

The majority of people in Thebes are barefoot as shoes are expensive. However, to really show wealth and status the well-turned-out Thebanite will invest in a pair of sandals. Sandals are, on the whole, straightforward and are produced with a flat sole the length of the foot with a thong that goes between the big toe and the second toe.

They are made from plant fibres, reeds or papyrus, although the latter are normally only seen on priests and the very rich. Men's sandals are generally twice the price of female ones and this is down primarily to the size. Leather sandals will have a longer lifespan than fibre sandals and would be worth investing in if walking features in your job; e.g. a soldier.

No matter how well made the sandals are you are likely at some point to have a shoe malfunction when the thong snaps, leaving the sole sitting in the mud. In every market there is someone who sells shoes and, more importantly, spare thongs, and they will fit it for you while you wait. This is an expensive repair and costs half the price of a new pair.

Decoration on Clothes

The majority of linen garments were left undyed to make washing easier as well as reflecting colourful jewellery. Tutankhamun, however, had a number of coloured garments heavy with decoration, including woven decoration, beads, discs and needlework.

One shawl, for example, was striped using bands of red and blue with a row of *ankhs* along the edge in brocade.

Tapestry was also used for decoration and a tunic from the tomb of Thutmosis IV (1419-1386 BCE) shows elaborate images of open and closed lotus flowers, birds and purple mandrakes.

Two of Tutankhamun's tunics have a fringe made of warp threads along the edge. Several are decorated with red, blue, green, yellow and white glass beads carefully stitched into a design. One tunic is decorated with gold discs, cylinder faience beads and plaques of gold and faience.

Other tunics in his tomb were decorated with appliqué and embroidery. One embroidered panel depicts a vulture, griffins and plant life. Another ankle-length tunic has a row of walking pin-tailed ducks along the bottom edge and around the collar is a row of flying pin-tailed ducks.

Another tunic bore embroidered panels of hunting scenes, griffins and sphinxes. The collar on this tunic was embroidered with a broad collar of floral design to resemble a necklace.

The neck lines and collars were also elaborately decorated in the tunics of the king and one has a vulture around the neck with the body in the middle of the back and the wings wrapped around the neck in protection.

All of these forms of decoration are likely to have been out of reach of the average Egyptian due to the cost to produce and also the difficulty in maintaining them.

Passing the Time in the Capital

Free-time is something that is valuable and generally only available to those who can afford not to work all daylight hours. It can be assumed that as you are reading this guide you are not only literate but also from the middle classes and therefore will have more free time than the average unskilled worker. Being in Kemet's capital city means you will be spoiled for things to do to entertain yourself and your family.

For the Children

Children's toys can be as expensive or as cheap as your budget dictates. Cost, however, does not detract from the pleasure a young child will get from them. The simplest and cheapest toys for younger children can be made from mud from the villages or from the banks of the Nile. Children love clay animals and these are easily fashioned, even by the children themselves. Popular at the moment are pigs, hippos, crocodiles, apes and humans. Of course you can go all out and provide boats[26] and chariots as well, if your modelling skills are up to the task. Your children will have hours of fun playing with these easily produced and easily replaced toys.

If you have a budget for children's toys, carpenters can be commissioned to produce articulated toys; i.e. toys with moveable parts. Animals are popular wooden toys; imagine the pleasure of a wooden cat with a moveable jaw controlled by a string, or a wooden mouse that squeaks.

For little girls, dolls are popular, and a carpenter can produce a realistic figure with moveable arms in a short period of time. However, this may be considered too much of an extravagance. In this instance someone handy with a needle could make a linen doll, and stuff it with straw and sand. To be even more creative and provide many more hours of fun, removable clothes can also be provided. There really are no limits to the quality of these dolls, and they can be commissioned from any woman in the village if your wife is not able to produce a suitable example.

Balls are by far the most common toy due to their versatility and there are numerous games that children can play with them. Again, depending on budget, balls can be made from a variety of materials; some are made of wood or clay, while others are made of strips of leather or plant fibre and papyrus wound tightly until the desired size ball is produced.

While many ball games come and go, there are some popular games that have been played since the Middle Kingdom (2040-1782 BCE). Juggling, for example, is a great pastime and can be played alone or as part of a competition. Often the practice of girls rather than boys, juggling is usually done with three balls and very skilled girls can do this while crossing and uncrossing their arms as they throw and catch the balls.

Another popular game for girls is piggy-back catch where two pairs compete against each other. One rides upon the other's back and throws the ball to the girl on the back from the other pair. When someone drops the ball they swap places.

Boys on the other hand have much more pent-up aggression and enjoy hitting a ball with a stick. One game involves a stick with a bend in it which is used to roll a ball along the ground, while a straight stick is used to hit the ball long distances.

Ritualistic Ball Games

In the eighteenth dynasty (1570-1293 BCE) there was a ritualistic ball game in which the king is shown hitting a ball with a stick or a club in the presence of the goddess Hathor, Mut, Sekhmet or Tefnut. He is shown with the stick in one hand and the ball in the other, indicating the ball was hit one-handed. There are two priests in the background whose role it was to retrieve the balls after they had been hit.

This ritual was representative of the destruction of the evil-eye of the snake god Apophis, the sworn enemy of the sun-god Ra.

A similar ritual may have been part of the sacred marriage between the king and the goddess depicted and there is a representation of this in the birth chamber at *ipt rshyt* (Luxor Temple). The goddess depicted, Hathor, is associated with love and the caption accompanying the scene talks of enjoyment and pleasure.

An example from the Late Period reign of Taharqa shows the king throwing a ball to each of the four cardinal points while running. This was part of a rejuvenation ceremony showing the king's power to rule.

The pointed-stick game is popular but with children running around without toe-coverings it can potentially be dangerous. This is also known as 'Territories' or 'Flashing Figures'. The game comprises a sharp, pointed stick – which the boys can fashion themselves – thrown at a marked target on the floor, or a sand-pit which is divided into squares representing the territories of each of the competitors. Each aims to get his stick into the territory of one of the competitors, at which point it is 'stolen' from them.

Boys in general prefer activities that demonstrate their strength, such as wrestling, weight-lifting or jumping. These activities stand them in good stead for a career in the army or a hard life on the farm.

Group Games

Generally, boys and girls are segregated in their play, even though in society they are not. Girls tend to do gentler activities such as dancing, juggling or acrobatics. There is more on dancing in the section on processions and evening entertainment.

A popular competitive sport played by boys is a hurdles game, called 'Jumping over the Goose' where two boys sit opposite each other with their feet and hands touching, creating a hurdle for other boys to jump over. To make the jump more difficult the boys sitting down widen their arms and legs so that the jumper has to jump higher and longer. You will often be walking through the village and hear the sound of young voices calling 'sit tight, here I come, friend!'[27]

A few games, though, are played by girls and boys together; for example the spinning or star game. This is also locally known as 'Erecting the Wine Arbour'. The boys stand in the centre and the girls hold their hands, lean back and let them swing them round and round until they get dizzy.[28]

The donkey game is often played between different age groups with an older child on hands and knees carrying two to four younger children on their back like the saddle bags on a pack animal. The young children riding the 'donkey' hold hands to prevent themselves from falling off.

Adult Entertainment

While there are plenty of activities to keep an adult busy in Thebes these are generally aimed towards men rather than women as men have more free time. Women who do not have paid employment (see section above) will be required to work in the home, preparing meals, looking after the children, producing clothes to sell at the market and generally taking care of the home. Unlike most jobs held by men, this does not finish when Ra dips beneath the western horizon. Women are generally working from the moment they wake up until the moment they go to sleep. Men on the other hand have more time to spend on idle pastimes.

Athletics

Popular with a lot of younger men are athletics and sports. Although this does form part of military training, non-military personnel often participate, especially if there is an opportunity to have a small wager, or as a demonstration of their strength.

Such demonstrations may be in the form of running long distances. This forms part of military training as soldiers are expected to cover long distances across deserts and rough terrain carrying equipment. Running across the desert is also great training if you enjoy hunting; chasing the quarry on foot is a particular skill.

There are no official events or competitions for running but that is not to say that they do not happen. On the scheduled days off from work in the village it is likely that there are impromptu contests between runners. As said earlier, Thebanites love to gamble.

Dashur Running Stela

The only evidence of an official race comes from the Dahshur running stela (685 BCE) discovered on the desert road leading to Dahshur, about 40km (25 miles) south of Cairo, in 1977. The stela records a race of army units which were tasked with running from Memphis to the Faiyum, covering a distance of 90km (56 miles).

They ran the first half at night, in order to avoid the heat, and the fastest completed it in four hours, resting in the Faiyum for two hours before returning to Memphis. The time taken to run the second half of the race was not recorded. King Taharka accompanied the runners in a chariot and even dismounted to join in the run for an hour.

There was a feast in Memphis for the finishers of the race, and the winner received praise from the king. All finishers also received unspecified prizes from the king.

Swimming

Although Thebes is on the river Nile and is in fact completely dependent on it for trade, transport, food and, to a certain extent, sport (see section on hunting below), swimming is not something that has a sporting or competitive element. Most people in Thebes, from royalty to peasant, are able to swim and in the popular *Five Tales of Wonder*[29] literary tale, the lover of the scribe's wife was known to swim in the lake after love-making (although ultimately it led to his demise). The dangers associated with swimming in the Nile could be why casual swimming, as opposed to practical swimming, is not that popular.

Those who swim regularly are generally fishermen, bird-catchers and militia; i.e., people with little choice in the matter. The Nile is a dangerous place. There are fast currents, hidden crocodiles and wallowing hippos, not to mention some nasty parasites that can be picked up from swimming in the more secluded branches and canals.

Competitive swimming, however, does appear in the religious tale of the *Quarrel of Horus and Seth*, a fantastic tale of good versus evil. In one of the sections there is an underwater swimming contest where the two gods turn themselves into hippos and propose to plunge into the depths of the Nile and stay submerged for a period of three months. They were, unfortunately, unable to complete their contest as Isis decided to cast her hook into the water to save her son Horus. You may find such swimming contests in your village, although you will not be expected to submerge for months at a time. If you are a keen swimmer perhaps you could start one, but be very aware of the dangers.

Messing Around in Boats

Whilst swimming is not necessarily a pastime for the wealthy, rowing and sailing most certainly are. In fact, boating on the Nile is such an important means of spending a pleasurable hour that the famous *Five Tales of Wonder* describe King Seneferu himself taking a pleasure trip on his lake while being rowed by a number of beautiful women dressed in nothing but fishnet dresses. Most people will not have such glamorous assistants and will have to row the boat themselves, or hire a boatman to do the hard work.

In general, any boat races in the Theban area will be low-key and organised in individual villages, although the great king, Amenhotep II (1453-1419 BCE) held a magnificent boat race where it is rumoured that 200 crew steered the boat for three *iteru* (32km/20 miles).

Boat jousting, tomb of Iymery, Giza.

Amenhotep's Sphinx Stela boasts of this boat race as well as his own skills in horsemanship and archery. Whether the king actually did the rowing is unlikely. Instead, he probably took the divine steering position, reminiscent of the king's role in the solar barque of the sun-god Ra.

If formal boat races are not for you, then it is recommended that you look out for the fishermen jousting that takes places on the Nile. This sport is not centrally organised and will come about when two 'rival' fishing boats come into contact with each other. The fishermen taunt each other and then try to push or hit their rivals with their long punting poles. Falling into the water is perilous, and it is inevitable that at least one fisherman won't be able to swim. Be warned, though, the language used is ripe and perhaps it may be advisable to keep the kids away from such spontaneous events.

Public Displays and Competitions

In the villages you may also come across impromptu wrestling matches as a show of strength, a fight to wager a bet or a demonstration of military skills. There are many opportunities for a flutter if you know where to

Soldiers wrestling, Luxor Museum.

look. Wrestling may even be presented to the public alongside dance and stick fighting as a public demonstration of strength, skill and stamina. If you come across such a demonstration it is best to keep out of the way, and do not volunteer for anything.

Wrestling is the main training activity of the military, but it has been adopted by the general public and has remained a popular tradition since the fifth dynasty (2498-2345 BCE). Traditionally, men wrestle naked as this provides a fairer fight as there are no items of clothing to grab hold of. However, in modern times more and more wrestlers are wearing short kilts and a broad belt, which would be used to provide a hand hold. Expect to see great feats of strength with at least one competitor being held upside down by the waist by his rival.

Wrestling is not monitored by the state or a guild, and therefore the rules are pretty flexible. Participants can grab any part of their partner's anatomy and the wrestling match is won when a competitor is unable to continue.

Another demonstration of strength and combat skills is the traditional art of stick fighting. This goes back to the time of the pyramids and is a skill attributed to the god Horus. It has recently become a display sport and you may come across people practicing or demonstrating their skills in the villages. Trainee fighters or those practicing will use soft papyrus stalks to try the technique. Wooden sticks are generally only used for public display, or military fighting.

A bout starts with the competitors bowing to the audience, and they will either fight with a stick in each hand or a stick in one hand and a wrist guard on the other arm. Referees will often be on hand to help score the match.

Watching the military train is another means of passing the time. Soldiers are known to have archery competitions, which demonstrate their prowess with a composite bow while riding a chariot. They will also throw arrows at wooden or copper targets while riding chariots at speed. They are all hoping to reach the skill levels of Thutmosis III who, 'when he shot at the target the wood splintered like papyrus.' The talents of Amenhotep II, son of Thutmosis III, far outstripped those of his father and it is recorded that 'he drew his bow whilst holding four arrows together in his fist. Thus he rode northwards shooting at them [the targets] … each arrow coming out at the back of his target while he attacked the next post.'[30]

Amenhotep III practising archery from a chariot, Luxor Museum. (Photograph by the author).

In their attempts to better these kings, the soldiers put on a very good display, which is well worth taking the time to watch. If possible, try to catch a chariot race at the site of Kom el 'Abd near Malkata, the palace of Amenhotep III. These races tend to be for the elite and royalty but it may be possible to get invited to watch, if you get to know the right people or work in the right industry. If you are able to get to the rest house at Kom el 'Abd it may be possible to glimpse the king as he watches the race, which is situated on a desert plain very close to the race road. This road starts about 2km (1¼ miles) from the edge of the desert and runs in a straight line to the base of the hills (Kola el-Hamra) 4km (2½ miles) away.

These are perfect opportunities to witness a high-calibre race with the elite of the army charioteering corps. But be prepared. Despite the careful clearance of the road prior to each race, there can be fatal accidents if the chariots hit a stone while travelling at speed.

More low-key but no less challenging is a team tug of war.[31] Two teams of men face each other and, rather than use a rope as is more traditional elsewhere in the world, the teams hold onto each other's wrists and try to pull the other team over. To maintain balance, each man rests his toes against the leg of the man in front with his heel on the ground. Everyone encourages his team members with comments such as, 'Your arm is much stronger than he. Don't give into him,' or taunts the other team, 'My side is much stronger than yours. Hold them firmly, my friend.' Of course, there are also likely to be more colourful taunts being shouted so protect your children's ears.

DID YOU KNOW?

Unlike Roman and Greek cultures, the ancient Egyptians did not have central arenas or colosseums for public entertainment. But this does not mean that public entertainment did not happen. Excavations have not yet uncovered a public space, but with the desert literally on their doorsteps, temporary arenas could have been set up quickly and without leaving anything for archaeologists to find.

A rather obscure observation (and participation) sport which requires no equipment is jumping. Competitors in contests are judged on how high they can jump with the winner being the person who jumps the highest. Generally the jumps are from a flat-footed stationery position and requires strong legs.

This sport gained momentum after featuring in the recent (New Kingdom) story of the *Tale of the Doomed Prince*. In this tale, the king of Naharin locked his daughter in a high tower and whoever could jump to her window could marry her. The local lads all tried: 'for three months now we are here passing the time in leaping. For he who reaches the window of the daughter of the Prince of Naharin will get her as a wife.' A passing Egyptian, who was the son of an officer, watched the jumping for a few days and then on his first try, 'He leaped, he reached the window of the daughter of the Prince of Naharin. She kissed him, she embraced him on all his body.' Naturally, the Egyptians excel at this sport, or at least feel heartened enough at the story to believe they do and it is an entertaining way of passing an idle hour.

Jumping is also seen in Thebes as a skill associated with fertility and the god Min. From the time of the pyramids, jumping and pole climbing has been a religious ritual, which you may be lucky enough to witness although they often take place within the temple. In the ritual four long poles are propped against a central pole with a number of men holding ropes on either side to keep the structure stable. The participants have to reach the top of the poles and the quickest is the winner. The key to success it taking a running jump at the start and therefore starting at a higher point on the poles. The men holding the ropes, however, have been known to destabilise, rather than stabilise the poles, making the task much more challenging.

Hunting and Fishing

Hunting and fishing are popular pastimes for the elite members of Theban society, and a necessary occupation of the poorer members of society who have to provide food. Though there are different hunting and fishing techniques for food catching and for entertainment, any animals killed on a hunt are eaten, whether they are hunted for pleasure or not, as meat is too valuable to waste.

Thebes, like every other town and city in Kemet, is surrounded by desert, which is teaming with wild animals. These include lions, leopards, ostriches, antelopes, deer, gazelle and desert bulls. It is believed by many local Thebanites that the hunter absorbs some of the main characteristics of the prey they kill, so the pressure is on to kill something impressive.

Larger game such as lions and desert bulls are generally preserved for the king, but for the more adventurous hunter it is possible to hunt hippopotamus in the Nile. Hippos are very dangerous and a worthy adversary for the river hunter. Traditionally they are hunted using spears and harpoons thrown from a boat or papyrus skiff for the particularly talented hunter.

Most desert game, though, is hunted using bows and arrows from the back of a chariot – should the hunter be lucky enough to have one – or on foot. The skills required are many and these need to be considered when deciding to join a desert hunt. Foot hunters need to be able to run for long distances, and chariot hunters need to be able to shoot arrows while moving.

Royal Hunting

New Kingdom pharaohs were prolific hunters; at least according to the propaganda records they commissioned.

Thutmosis III (1504-1450 BCE) is recorded as killing 120 elephants for their ivory on a single hunt, a rhino with a single arrow, and twelve wild bulls in a single hour. He was a man to be feared.

Amenhotep III (1386-1349 BCE) issued commemorative hunting scarabs and claims to have killed 110 lions and ninety-six bulls with his own arrows.

What the kings fail to record is that these hunts were a team effort. The animals were 'ambushed' by a line of hunters, beaters and dogs going ahead to flush the animals out. Then when they were cornered the king had a clear shot. Sometimes the animals were even placed into a penned area to ensure the king's success.

Fishing, like hunting, can be a practical activity or a leisure activity for the upper-middle classes. The practicalities of the activity are different depending on the objective. For example, fishermen whose job is to catch as many fish as possible per day, generally work as a team and cast nets into the water to catch dozens of fish in one go. Fishing for pleasure is more skilled, but ultimately you may not end up with many, if any, fish to take home at the end of the day.

Someone taking a day trip fishing in the marshes or on the Nile will need to use a spear rather than fishing nets. The fisherman will stand upon a papyrus skiff or shallow-bottomed boat, and plunge it into the water in order to spear a fish. It is a lot harder than it looks.

If fishing with a spear is not proving successful, the intrepid marsh hunter can have a go at fowling, which comprises catching marsh birds using a throw-stick. It is stated that it is possible to 'trap birds by the thousands in this manner', but this is an exaggeration. Standing on the same shallow-bottomed papyrus skiff, birds are flushed out of the marshes and then stunned or killed by throwing a curved throw-stick at them. The birds are then retrieved and can be taken home to be eaten.

In fact, fishing and fowling is becoming such a popular pastime for the upper-middle classes that a text has just been written called *The*

Pleasures of Fishing and Fowling (1570-1293 BCE) which describes the joy and pleasure attained through these activities:

> I cannot remain far from the people after whom my heart hankers, my friends. I would like to spend the day in the place of my yearnings. When day breaks I would like to eat, to be far away, to go to my favourite place.

It is considered an activity for the whole family, although naturally it is only the man in the family who will actually spear the fish and throw the sticks. The family are there simply to keep the man company in the boat and share the pleasures of being in the marshes.

If fishing and fowling in the marshes is too precarious and potentially dangerous then pool fishing may be the right activity for you. This is something you can do if you have a home large enough to incorporate a fish pool. If this is the case you can relax on a low stool with a fishing rod and a drink and some snacks to hand. It is a very relaxed and civilised way of whiling away an afternoon and, of course, it is easier to catch a fish in the confines of a pool than in the river.

If you do not have a private pool to fish in, rod-fishing in a canal is a possibility and adds a little more challenge to catching the fish. Furthermore, you will not have to pay to replace them as you would if you were fishing from your own private pool. Fishing with a rod is aided by the use of copper or bone fish-hooks, some of which are barbed, ensuring the fish is firmly secured on the line. This can also be a family activity, with the man of the house holding and casting the rod and his wife keeping him company and removing the fish from the hook.

Board Games

One of the easiest and most lucrative ways of passing the time is by playing board games. People of all ages play them and while it is lovely to have a fancy board, you will see people playing games with impromptu boards carved into stone pavements, or drawn in the sand and by using small pebbles as dancers or gaming pieces. This is, in fact, all that is needed to have a quick game with a fellow villager.

DID YOU KNOW?

Dice as we know it did not exist until the Graeco-Roman period of Egyptian history. Prior to this period throw-sticks or knuckle bones were used instead.

Throw-sticks had one dark and one light side, and the combination of light and dark sides once they were thrown determined the number of places to be moved. Knuckle bones – from a sheep or goat – worked in the same way. Sometimes carved ivory versions were used instead. They had four distinct faces – flat, concave, convex and twisted – and once thrown the combination determined the number of spaces the dancer could be moved.

Senet

The most popular game at the moment is senet, which is also known as 'The Game of Passing' and has been played by the people of Kemet since the first dynasty (2686-2613 BCE). If you are new to the game be aware the people of Thebes have been playing this for over 1,000 years. Don't bet too heavily!

Senet is a game played on thirty squares, or 'houses', arranged in three rows of ten squares each. There are two players with between five and seven dancers each; one player has cones and the other has reels. The objective of this game of strategy is to move all the dancers through the thirty squares – switching direction at the end of each row – to the end while also trying to knock your opponent's pieces off the board.

Some houses, marked with hieroglyphs, identify either a lucky or unlucky square which can either be a blessing or a curse to land on. For example, square fifteen is the 'frog' or 'house of rebirth' and is considered a lucky square whereas square sixteen, the 'net', and square twenty-seven, 'the waters of chaos', are both unlucky squares. The final five squares hold the sequence good-bad-three-two-one. The latter three represent different deities and are the final squares the player needs to pass to finish the game.

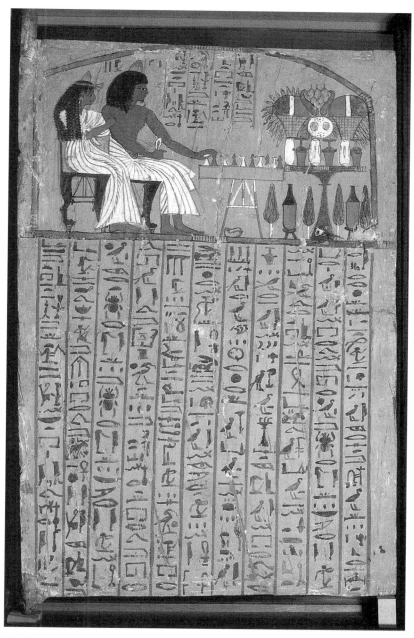

Playing Senet from the tomb of Sennedjem, Deir el Medina. (Photograph courtesy of Wikicommons Media, Mamienefer).

In recent years the popularity of senet has led to its inclusion in funerary rituals, and chapter seventeen from the *Book of the Dead* shows the deceased playing an unseen opponent to secure their place in the afterlife. The stakes are not so high in a village game of senet.

Twenty-Squares

On the rear of most senet boards – if you are fortunate to own a board – is the board for the game 'twenty squares' which is simpler than senet but no less entertaining. The board is set out in a four-twelve-four formation, with every fourth square on the long row marked with a rosette or hieroglyphs. The game is played with two players with five 'dancers' each.

Dogs and Jackals

Another popular game is hounds and jackals. It has been played now for about 1,000 years so is well established as a village pastime. The boards can be in various forms – some plaque shaped and some animal shaped – although it is possible to play by scratching a board in the sand if no other alternative is available. Each board has thirty holes for each of the two players, including one extra-large hole at the end of the board.[32] Expensive boards include a drawer underneath to store the gaming pieces.

Each player has five pins which stand up in the holes; these pins bear the head of either a dog or a jackal. The object of the game is for each of the two players to move all five pins from one end of the board into the large hole. Each player takes it in turns to move and the number of spaces moved is determined by throwing the knuckle bones or casting sticks. As with senet, there are some obstacles along the way, with some holes joined to others enabling the player to jump forward. Holes six and twenty and eight and ten are joined by lines, so if you land in any of these you will have to follow the line to the other hole, which could be a negative or a positive thing depending on where you are in the game. Holes fifteen and twenty-five are 'safe havens' and are identified by a *nefer* sign, so this is a good hole to land in.

This game is much simpler to play than senet but still worth a small flutter as strategy and cunning are the keys to winning.

DID YOU KNOW?

Whilst board games have been discovered in ancient Egypt from settlement and funerary sites, sometimes complete with gaming pieces and knuckle bones or casting sticks, not one set of rules has been discovered. Archaeologists and game theorists have come up with rudimentary sets of rules for each game found but no one knows if these were the rules by which the Egyptians played.

Evening Entertainment

Evening entertainment is not lacking in Thebes although there are few, if any, official get togethers other than the regular religious festivals. However, as soon as you have settled in and made some friends you will be invited to house parties and informal gatherings in the village. These will inevitably include music, singers and dancers, with varying levels of professionalism depending on budget.

People of the Nile valley love music and singing and you will be able to hear singing throughout the day, with workmen, fishermen, farmers and women by the river singing to help pass the time or add rhythm to the work they are doing. Unfortunately, the lyrics to many of these daily work songs are improvised and therefore not recorded for you to learn. If you listen carefully you will be able to pick up the lyrics, but beware that fishermen's songs can be quite fruity.

For private parties, weddings, funerary rituals and religious processions, professional groups of singers, dancers and musicians are available to hire. Most middle to upper class banquets and parties will include a dance troupe accompanied by musicians. Musicians can be male or female and include a variety of instruments including lutes, harps, clappers and flutes, with percussionists on drums and tambourines or someone clapping to keep the rhythm. Dancers are invariably female and often wear little more than a belt and a wig. They are often part of travelling dance troupes who move from village to village, so if there is one troupe in particular that you like you may have to wait for it to return to Thebes.

Love Songs

A number of love songs have survived from the New Kingdom, but it is unknown if they were sung, recited or read as literary works. They may very well have been sung at banquets and have been well-known enough that everyone participated.

The love songs vary in style and length and the narrators could be male or female. Many talk of unrequited love but are useful for learning about cultural practices and ideas surrounding love and romance, as well as idealised images of beauty.

> He is neighbour to my mother's house,
> And I cannot go to him!
> Mother is right in charging him thus: "Give up seeing her."
> It pains my heart to think of him,
> I am possessed by love of him.
> Truly, he is a foolish one,
> But I resemble him;
> He knows not my wish to embrace him,
> Or he would write to my mother.[33]

Dancers in Thebes are also acrobats and many performances include backflips, handstands and cartwheels, with lots of rapid head movements causing the hair to move in a pleasing manner. It is said that many dancers weight their hair or wigs in order to aid with the movement while performing. The *ib* dance in particular focuses on the hair as a prop in the routine and all the dancers attach balls to their hair and drag them along the ground in time to the music. A skilled dancer can enthral an audience just by flicking her hair.

It is very unusual for male and female dancers to dance together, but there are both male and female dance troupes with a very traditional male dance of the Old Kingdom known as *tjeref*. Generally when dances are performed in pairs, they are same sex and their moves mirror each other.

Music is so important to Thebans that some large households employ a solitary harpist, often blind, to entertain them privately. Blind harpists are in great demand and are paid well. It is very unusual to see a thin blind harpist.

While many women from the upper-middle classes may be able to play a harp or a flute it is not considered appropriate for them to entertain in public, regardless of how talented they may be. However, although noble women do not perform in public, music and dance is so important to Theban society and wider Kemet that there are at least four deities associated with music: Bes Hathor, Ihy, and Thoth.

Music is believed to have been created by Thoth, the god of wisdom, and therefore is an important aspect of temple worship, religious processions and rituals (see section on processions and female employment). Female musicians in a religious context can often be seen shaking the *sistrum* (sacred rattle) and the *menat* (a

Acrobatic dancers from the tomb of Khety, Beni Hasan, (Drawing after Decker 1992, fig. 110).

Blind Harpist from the New Kingdom tomb of Nakht. (Photograph courtesy of Wikicommons Media, Yorck Prokject).

beaded necklace) while a songstress accompanies by singing prayers and hymns. Temple musicians are held in similar esteem within the society as a priest or priestess, more so than professional dancers performing at banquets.

You will not be able to stay in Thebes for long before you are entertained by music, song or dance and you will quickly be caught up in the musicality of the villagers.

Obeying the Laws of Maat

Unlike countries outside of the boundaries of Kemet, there is no form of codified law which joins all the *nomes* of Kemet together. Instead, each town, and *nome* has their own set of acceptable laws, which are dealt with on a case-by-case basis.

DID YOU KNOW?

The earliest set of laws comes from the Ptolemaic Period, after the invasion of Alexander the Great (332 BCE). Even at this time these laws are more like a 'practitioner's handbook' than a code of law reference book.

Most of the evidence of the legal system in earlier periods comes from Deir el Medina in the New Kingdom in the form of a list of cases. Often the end of the text is missing and therefore the punishment is lost.

One nineteenth-dynasty (1293-1185 BCE) papyrus, lists stolen property and the level of fine that the thief was ordered to make:

List of property stolen by the female servant of the charioteer Pekhari:

One bronze wash-basin; twenty deben, penalty forty deben of copper.

One bronze vessel; six deben, penalty eighteen deben of copper.

One bronze spittoon; six deben, penalty eighteen deben of copper.

Two garments of fine cloth; penalty six deben of copper.

This method of fining double or even triple the cost of the stolen item is supported by other similar case records and could therefore be assumed to be the standard penalty. In a society without a monetary system, and therefore no means of saving, large penalties could also be paid back in man-hours.

The Kenbet

The *kenbet* or court is the official route for pursuing justice for a crime committed against you, and comprises a number of local individuals who sit with the vizier to hear the appeals.

One *kenbet* is in the village of the Place of Truth (Deir el Medina) and consists of sixteen seats, occupied by the same sixteen men week after week. This is only available to the people who live in the village. A more accessible *kenbe*t is outside of the gate area of the temple of Khonsu at Karnak, in an open square. Other *kenbets* may meet in local villages as and when they are required, so if you need advice locate your nearest one.

The *kenbet* is not there to 'find out the truth' but rather to maintain public order by whatever means possible. This sometimes means going with general public opinion regarding the penalties for a crime. To be safe in Thebes it is a very good idea to be amenable to the people in your village and workplace, as annoying the wrong people can end up with a tougher punishment than a crime warrants.

The *kenbet* works under the watchful eye of the goddess Maat, the goddess of truth and justice, although the vizier is ultimately in charge. Although their role is not to find out the truth, honest testament is taken very seriously. There are harsh penalties if a defendant lies to the *kenbet* and perjury is often considered more serious than the crime itself.

The *kenbet*, to a certain extent, is happy to trust people on their word and to accept oaths from defendants stating they will not commit an offence again as good enough to conclude a case; in fact this is the most common way for a case to end.

Should a defendant go against their own oath, or fail to pay a fine incurred, the *kenbet* do not take it lightly. The oaths are technically made to the gods and to the king in the presence of the vizier and the *kenbet* and by breaking them they are bringing the wrath of the gods and the king upon their heads.

The vizier's role in the *kenbet* is a very powerful one and can easily be abused. If you are unable to befriend the vizier and you end up in front of the *kenbet* a discrete bribe might be worth considering. The vizier literally has the life and death of everyone who appears before him in his hands. Not only can he administer the death penalty, but he can also affect the lives of the condemned family for generations.

Families can be held responsible for the acts of individuals and they are not permitted to profit from the illegal gains of a criminal. Therefore, a criminal and his family are often sentenced to lifelong labour together as state-owned slaves if their crime is considered severe enough. In some instances of high-ranking defendants, not only could they lose their position as punishment but this could be extended to the entire family, resulting in a loss of a home as well as an income.

Teti

A seventeenth-dynasty (1663-1570 BCE) temple official called Teti was found guilty of an unspecified crime. Not only did he lose his position but also he was: 'expelled from the temple of my father Min, and let him be removed from the position in the temple, from son to son, from heir to heir.'

In a culture where positions were passed on from son to son, this punishment not only affected Teti and his immediate family but also his descendants for many generations.

Classifying something as a crime can be rather arbitrary and it is useful to know that often an incident is only considered a crime if the injured party wishes to pursue it. As you can probably imagine, keeping on the good side of your work colleagues and neighbours is advisable, as vindictive people can ensure you are punished for a crime; even one you have not committed.

So, for example, theft is only a crime when the injured party chooses to pursue it. Often stolen items are simply ordered to be restored to the original owner and sometimes a little compensation added for good measure.

State Crimes

The only clear crimes – every time without fail – are those that involve the state or the temple. Any crime against these institutions is officially pursued and investigated by the vizier and his office and results in more severe punishments.

Sexual Crimes

Sexual crimes, such as adultery, seduction or rape, are only pursued as a crime if the injured party – generally the husband of the woman – wishes to pursue the perpetrator. The punishment for these crimes is inconsistent and depends on the perseverance of the injured husband.

Seduction or rape of unmarried girls is likely to end up in the girl being forced into marriage in order to avoid any unnecessary scandal as a priority over prosecuting the man.

Adultery in general is not a crime, although an enraged husband may attempt to kill the adulterous man. The officials of the *kenbet* tend to get involved mainly to keep public order and to restrict the behaviour of the cuckolded husband. However, bear in mind that a revenge murder by the cuckolded husband is not considered socially unacceptable. The husband can pursue his revenge but within the limits of public order.

Death by Magic

In the Middle Kingdom *Five Tales of Wonder*, one of the stories concerns the wife of a scribe who commits adultery.

> They spent a day in the summer house, and feasted there, and in the evening the youth bathed in the lake. The chief butler then went to his master and informed him what had come to pass.

The scribe called for a magician to come to help him solve the problem of his adulterous wife.

On another day, when the scribe dwelt with Pharaoh, the lovers were together in the summer house, and at eventide the youth went into the lake. The butler stole through the garden, and stealthily he cast into the water the wax image, which was immediately given life. It became a great crocodile that seized the youth suddenly and took him away.

With the lover out of the way, the scribe wanted his wife to be punished.

Then Pharaoh gave command that the wife of the scribe should be seized. On the north side of the house she was bound to a stake and burned alive, and what remained of her was thrown into the Nile.

Both of them were denied a burial and an afterlife as their bodies had been cast into the water without mummification or a funeral.

As the injured party in a sexual crime is considered to be the husband, it will come as no surprise that women and men were treated very differently under the *kenbet* system. While a wife and her children can lose their freedom and be punished with forced labour due to the crimes of her husband, this does not happen in reverse. A man would not lose his freedom due to the crimes of his wife.

Hard Labour

As one would expect, those destined for hard labour have a particularly rough time, especially if sent to the mines or quarries. The journey to get there is arduous and it is uncertain whether they will safely reach their destination or not.

The routes to the quarries and mines are through desert lands that are particularly difficult due to the lack of water. Although soldiers accompanying them are generally able to identify sites and dig wells successfully it is recorded that, 'Whenever the gold prospectors went there it was only ever half of them that arrived, for they died of thirst on the way, along with their donkeys.'[34]

The fear of being sent for forced labour in the mines and quarries is so great amongst the people of Thebes it is common to say as an oath: 'If I am lying may I be mutilated and sent to the quarries.'

Home and Away

As a newcomer to Kemet, if you end up in court you may end up with a harsher punishment than an Egyptian. There was a recent case of a rebellion comprising Egyptian protagonists who were given a trial with the vizier and the *kenbet* before being issued with the death sentence. However, rebellions by non-Egyptians, such as Nubians in Egyptian-occupied Nubia, result in no trial. If the death penalty is issued, they are executed publically to prevent further rebellion. The bodies are typically denied a proper burial and pinned to the walls of the fort they rebelled against.

This scenario is unlikely to relate to an expat in Thebes but it might be worth considering that outsiders are treated differently.

If a crime is committed where death is not the appropriate punishment a non-Egyptian could be transported to Egypt as a prisoner, conscripted into the army or sent for hard labour. This is not much different than Egyptians committing state crimes. However, such a punishment may not be all bad as foreign prisoners can be rewarded for loyalty by being placed in a domestic household, where they can, ultimately, earn their freedom, get married and raise a family.

The Oracle

The oracle has been addressed in the section on religion but it is a vital part of the legal system in Kemet. As mentioned, religion intertwines with every aspect of daily life.

Any person accused of a crime can appeal directly to the oracle of a god of their choice rather than to the vizier. There are better odds of getting the decision or judgement of their choice using this process. Although one would expect the word and judgment of god to be finite. It is not. The accused can ask as many oracles as he/she wishes as many times as required until a judgement is accepted by them.

There are rumours of one workman from the Place of Truth (Deir el Medina) who ignored the oracle judgment on five occasions from three different gods. He was finally coerced through public opinion and a beating to admit to the crime, accept responsibility for it and accept the judgement of the oracle.

Death Penalty

The death penalty is given for crimes against the state, the king or the gods. Such crimes could include perjury, which, as discussed above, could be seen as a crime against the gods and the king. For a particularly heinous crime the accused will be sentenced to death, followed by deprivation of the burial rights. This ensures that they are cast into oblivion for eternity.

Execution is more common than many people would like. The only person who can overthrow a vizier's judgement is the king, under whom he was working, but it is rare for the king to intervene. It seems they leave such distasteful things to the vizier to deal with.

Harem Conspiracy

The king tended to separate himself from the death penalty, and in the case of the harem conspiracy, Ramses III (1182-1151 BCE), in a document about the court case, states:

> I spoke to them strictly saying: "Take care, in case you should allow an innocent man to be punished by an official who is not his superior." This I said to them repeatedly. As for all this that has been done, it is they who have done it. May the blame fall on their heads while I am safeguarded, exempted forever, for I am amongst the just kings before Amun-Re.

Although the people being condemned to death had conspired to kill the king, for which the penalty is death, the king keeps it at arm's length, as if he does not want his soul tarnished with the possibility of a wrong conviction.

Execution is carried out by impaling on a wooden stake. If the wood pierces the heart or a major blood vessel the death is quick, but if the wood misses all the major organs then death is very slow and painful.

If possible the criminal is executed near to the place where they committed the crime – if the death penalty was issued for stealing from a temple they would be executed near the temple – and in public as a deterrent to other would-be thieves. However, although they take place in public, executions are not considered a public holiday and people do not gather to watch it as a spectator sport.

Death by fire has been another common method of execution since the Middle Kingdom (2040-1782 BCE) and there are plenty of cases of when this has been the punishment for various crimes. In the Middle Kingdom, Neferhotep explains on his funerary stela that the common punishment for misuse of the cemetery at Abydos was being destroyed by fire. The inscription at the temple of Tod by king Senusret I (1971-1926 BCE) explains that those who vandalise temples 'have been placed on the brazier'. However, this method of execution is not just for major crimes; one man, accused of stealing three state-owned chisels, was executed by being 'thrown into the fire'.

In a situation like this, it would also be common for a workman to be sent into the criminal's pre-prepared tomb (should he have one) to chisel out any references to his name. This ensures the name cannot be repeated, or aid in their afterlife in any way. A truly eternal punishment.

Crime Cases

We are lucky enough to have records of real crimes that were presented before the *kenbet* and the punishments that were administered for each crime. These are all dated to the New Kingdom.

Sety is accused by the scribe, Neferhotep, on behalf of the state, of misusing the staff at the temple of Abydos for his own purposes. He was sentenced to 200 blows and five open wounds, plus repayment of work days lost.

Merysekhmet had been having an affair with a woman who was engaged to be married; he himself was also married. The woman's fiancé already brought this accusation to the court and Merysekhmet swore an oath to the vizier that he would never see her again or he would be mutilated and have his ears and nose cut off and sent to Kush in exile.

However, he continued to see her and she became pregnant. When in front of the *kenbet* he swore another oath to say he would not see her again on pain of being sent to the quarries in Nubia for a life of hard labour.

In another case Sese was accused of trying to increase the boundaries of his agricultural field by moving the fencing between his field and that of the neighbouring temple of Amun. For this crime of stealing land from the state Sese was sentenced to amputation of the nose and ears and loss of freedom for his wife and children.

Shopping

In Thebes, as in any other town or village in Kemet, there will be a regular market. This is not necessarily at a designated place, as there are very few public squares in Thebes, but market stalls gather along the banks of the river Nile on a regular basis and other sellers gather by the sycamores on the west bank (you may need to ask directions if you get lost). The market is essentially a gathering of people who have items to sell and people who wish to buy.

The market is not the only means of shopping as all sellers will sell from their homes or workshops, or work on commission.

Without regulated shops and no monetary system, shopping is a complicated and time-consuming activity. In a community with a barter system it is essential that you pay what the goods are worth, and what you are happy to pay for them. If you are not happy with the exchange offered then remember you can always walk away, regardless of how enthusiastic the salesman or woman is.

Every item you could possibly want has a standard market value and it would be useful as a newcomer to the system to learn what some of the comparable values are so you are exchanging like for like. Most items are given a market value in *deben* of copper, grain or silver, although these things do not have to be exchanged for the required item so long as the items amount to the same market value. If you are paying in metal or grain be aware that not all sellers are honest. Note that when they weigh your payment to ensure it meets the price asked they do not always use the correct weights. Be aware of the value of the items you have to exchange.

Exchange Rates

In Kemet there is a complex system of value which seems impenetrable to outsiders, but people know the value of each item in the same way that all modern societies do. For example, you would know a loaf of bread does not have the same market value as a pair of gold earrings. In Kemet it is the same.

The most common values are known as *deben* of copper, which equates to approximately 91g. For oil there is a measurement known as a *hin*, which is about 0.48l and is approximately the same value as one *deben*. High-end items are valued using *kite* of silver; ten *kite* is approximately one *deben* or 91g.

Liquids are also sold in jars, wood is sold in bundles, and organic material is sold in lumps.

However, although there is a strict system, items are only as valuable as the buyer thinks they are. If there is only one tunic and you need a tunic then the price will soar if you express great need. As in any society, the demand affects the cost.

Although shopping in the market is a 'learn on the job' kind of activity here is a list of the cost of the most common items you are likely to want to purchase. Bear in mind the costs are guides only as it is a supply and demand economy. Prices vary depending on how popular an item is as well as how desperately someone wants to sell something or how desperately someone wants to buy something.

Food

Bread	2 deben (10 loaves)
	5 deben (25 loaves)
	3 deben (120 cakes)
Beer	½ deben (1 jar)
Wine	1 deben
Fish	2 deben (50 gutted fish)
Flour	8-16 deben
Wine	4 deben
Honey	50 deben
Vegetables	½ deben (70 bundles)
Salt	4 deben
Fresh fat	30 deben
Oil	1 deben
Wheat	1-2 deben (sack 58kg)
Barley	2 deben (sack)

Clothes

Tunic	5 deben
Skirt	11-30 deben (dependant on quality)
Triangular loincloth	4-16 deben
Cloak	50 deben
Sandals	1-3 deben

Cosmetic items

Razor	1-2 deben
Mirror	6-15 deben
Ivory comb	2 deben
Cosmetic stick	1 deben
Amulet	1 deben

Livestock

Goat	1-3 deben
Bird	¼ deben
Donkey	25-40 deben
Cattle	20-140 deben
Pig	5-7 deben
Fowl	¼ deben
Jackal	1 deben
Cow (rental for one month)	4 artabas of wheat (1 artaba is about 38l)

Furniture

Bed	12-25 deben
Bed footboard	1 deben
Couch	2 deben
Footstool	2-3 deben
Seat	15-20 deben
Folded Stool	1-30 deben
Sleeping mat	2 deben

Glossary

akh ikr en re – Literally translated as an 'Excellent Spirit of Re', this refers to the deceased. They acquire powers when entering the afterlife which categorise them as demi-gods; not as powerful as traditional deities but powerful enough to interfere or intervene in the life of the living.

Barque – This is a sacred boat that could be used on the Nile during sacred river processions or carried upon the shoulders of the priests during the procession on land. The statue of the god was sealed inside a shine on the barque.

Deben – This is a weight of copper comparable to 91g. It was used as a relative value and people were not expected to go to the market with baskets full of copper to exchange, although this was of course an acceptable currency.

Going Forth by Day – This was a means of describing someone who had died and was starting the journey into the afterlife. The book more commonly referred to as *The Book of the Dead* is actually entitled *The Book of Going Forth by Day*.

Hieroglyphs – The picture writing found in temples and tombs. This script is phonetic in nature but signs can also be logographic and syllabic. This was used in a religious context.

Hieratic – This is the cursive form of hieroglyphs and is a form of shorthand. Hieratic was used for secular texts and therefore the majority of the information about everyday lives of the ancient Egyptians is written in hieratic.

Ka – The life force of an individual which stays with the individual from birth until death. Following death, if the correct rituals are carried out and offerings made, the deceased will live eternally.

Kenbet – The court system, which is similar to a modern jury, with sixteen men who listen to the cases and concerns of the villagers. Their role was not to find out the truth but to maintain peace.

Maat – This is the goddess of truth, justice and cosmic equilibrium. *Maat* is also used to describe the concept of law and justice. Maintaining the law of *Maat* was an important aspect of kingship as this ensured the stability of Egypt.

Medical Papyri – There are a number of papyri which have been discovered in ancient Egypt and these include lists of medical cases, diagnosis, and treatment. These papyri include the Ebers papyrus, Kahun Gynecological Papyrus, Chester Beatty and Hearst amongst others. They are invaluable for identifying medical practice in ancient Egypt.

Nome – Egypt was divided into administrative regions known as *nomes* which were governed by their own chieftain, laws and religious practices.

Opening of the Mouth – This ceremony ensured the deceased is able to continue eating, breathing and speaking in the afterlife by ceremoniously 'cutting' the mummy bandages with an adze.

Ostraca/ostracon (pl) – This is the name given to broken pot or limestone sherds which were used as notepaper. Hundreds of thousands of ostracon have been found in Deir el Medina and provide information on all aspects of life in Egypt, administrative records and literary texts.

Stela /Stelae (pl) – These are dome-topped slabs of stone, which are inscribed with a text. They can be religious or political and are placed generally at temples throughout Egypt. Smaller stelae are commissioned by ordinary people for funerary texts or for household worship.

The Golden – This was another name for the goddess Hathor.

True of Voice – When someone was dead they were referred to as True of Voice. In inscriptions this title follows the name of anyone who is deceased, rather like RIP, in order to make it clear who was alive and who was not.

Endnotes

1 This description is based on the smallest house footprint at the Middle Kingdom village of Kahun in the Faiyum.
2 Tutankhamun's tomb contains both the raw ingredients required for bread-making in the form of emmer wheat as well as loaves of baked bread.
3 One of the jars discovered at the palace of Malkata was labelled as 'blended.'
4 Inscriptions from residents of Deir el Medina.
5 More than 150 ancestor busts have been discovered, primarily from Deir el Medina.
6 An ostraca is a sherd of pottery or limestone which was commonly used as notepaper. These were picked up from the ground or from broken household tableware. They vary in size from a few centimetres to more than a metre long.
7 The practice is discussed in the sixth dynasty mastaba tomb at Saqqara of Nedjemib.
8 Ebers Papyrus dated to 1550 BCE.
9 Edwin Smith Papyrus dated to 1600 BCE but thought to have been copied from an earlier text.
10 These specific ingredients have not been identified.
11 Ebers Papyrus.
12 Edwin Smith Papyrus.
13 These may have had an element of antibacterial properties.
14 Ebers Papyrus.
15 Ebers Papyrus.
16 One skeleton, discovered in 2013 at Amarna, had suffered from a broken foot and femur, and was one of two skeletons wearing a copper alloy toe-ring, the only such items discovered in Egypt. It is thought they may have been worn to aid healing.

17 Edwin Smith Papyrus.

18 Modern research has shown there is evidence of quartz, greywacke, amphibole and mica grains in bread samples, which were possibly added to make grinding easier as the quantities discovered are likely to have entered naturally.

19 Studies by the Manchester Mummy Project found that on twenty-nine male mummies there were seventy-two abscesses and on twelve female mummies there were forty-five abscesses.

20 Ebers Papyrus.

21 Willow forms the basis of aspirin and may actually have worked.

22 Edwin Smith Papyrus.

23 From the Kahun Gynaecological Papyrus, which is the oldest medical papyrus in Egypt and dates to 1800 BCE.

24 Such medicinal use is emphasised on New Kingdom kohl pots which were used for the storage of eye cosmetics. Inscription from these pots include; 'Good for the sight', 'To staunch bleeding', 'To cause tears', or 'For cleaning the eyes'.

25 Both lipstick and rouge seems to have been introduced in the New Kingdom. The bust of Nefertiti shows her lips as darker than her face, indicating lipstick was used. In the nineteenth-dynasty tomb of Nefertari, the wife of Ramses II, her cheeks are shown with two darkened circles which could indicate rouge. A Middle Kingdom relief in the British Museum depicts a woman wiping her face with a small pad, which could demonstrate the application or removal of cosmetics.

26 Examples of these have been found in the Middle Kingdom village of Kahun.

27 In the fifth-dynasty tomb in Saqqara of the vizier Ptahhotep.

28 Middle Kingdom tomb of Baqet III at Beni Hasan.

29 Papyrus Westcar (P. Berlin 3033) dated to the Middle Kingdom.

30 Great Sphinx Stela of Amenhotep II at Giza.

31 This is recorded in the sixth-dynasty tomb of Mereruka in Saqqara.

32 In the twelfth-dynasty tomb of Reny-Seneb at Asasif in Thebes a shield-shaped example of hounds and jackals was discovered with a palm tree drawn down the centre. It was made of ivory and ebony and sycamore wood.

33 Papyrus Chester Beatty I, dated to the Ramesside Period.

34 During the reign of Ramses II (1279-1212 BCE) so a little later than the time period of this book.

Bibliography

Baines, J., and Malek, J., *Atlas of Ancient Egypt* (Facts on File, Oxford, 1980)

Bierbrier, M., *The Tomb Builders of the Pharaohs* (Charles Scribners Sons, New York, 1982)

Bjorkman, G., *Kings at Karnak* (Uppsala, Sweden, 1971)

Booth, C., *An Illustrated Guide to Ancient Egypt* (Amberley, Stroud, 2014)

Booth, C., *Ancient Egyptians for Dummies (*John Wiley, Bognor Regis, 2007)

Booth, C., *In Bed with the Egyptians* (Amberley, Stroud, 2015)

Booth, C., *The Nile and its People* (The History Press, Stroud, 2010)

Breasted, J.H., *Ancient Records of Egypt*. Vol II (University of Chicago Press. Chicago, 1906)

Černy, J., *A Community of Workmen at Thebes in the Ramesside Period* (Bibliotheque D'Etude, Cairo, 1973)

Clayton, P., *Chronicle of the Pharaohs* (Thames and Hudson, London, 1994)

Collier, M., and Quirke, S., *The UCL Lahun Papyri: Religious, Literary, Legal, Mathematical and Medical* BAR s1209 (Archaeopress, Oxford, 2004)

Corteggiani, J-P., *The Egypt of the Pharaohs at the Cairo Museum* Scala Books, London, 1986)

David, R., (Ed) *Egyptian Mummies and Modern Science* (Cambridge University Press, Cambridge, 2008)

David, R., and Tapp, E., *Evidence Embalmed: Modern Medicine and the Mummies of Ancient Egypt* (Manchester University Press, Manchester, 1984)

David, R., and Tapp, E., *The Mummy's Tale: The Scientific and Medical Investigation of Natsef-Amun, Priest in the Temple of Karnak* (Michael O'Mara books Ltd, London, 1992)

David, R., *Religion and Magic in Ancient Egypt* (Penguin, London, 2002)

David, R., *The Pyramid Builders of Ancient Egypt* (Guild Publishing, London, 1986)

David, R., (Ed) *Manchester Museum Mummy Project: Multidisciplinary Research on Ancient Egyptian Mummified Remains* (Manchester Museum Press, Manchester, 1979)

Davies, B., *Who's Who at Deir el Medina.* (Nederlands Instituut Voor Het Nabije Oosten, Leiden, 1999)

Dayagi-Mendels, M., *Perfumes and Cosmetics in the Ancient World* (The Israel Museum, Jerusalem, 1989)

Dodson, A., and Ikram, S., *The Mummy in Ancient Egypt; Equipping the Dead for Eternity* (Thames and Hudson, London, 1998)

Donker van Heel, K., *Djekhy and Son: Doing Business in Ancient Egypt* (American University in Cairo Press, Cairo, 2013)

Filer, J., *Disease (*British Museum Press, London, 1995)

Fletcher, J., *Chronicle of a Pharaoh; the Intimate Life of Amenhotep III* (Oxford University Press, Oxford, 2000)

Hall, R., *Egyptian Textiles* (Shire Egyptology. Risborough, 1986)

Hart, G., *A Dictionary of Egyptian Gods and goddesses (*Routledge, London, 1986)

Hornung, E., *The Ancient Egyptian Books of the Afterlife (*Cornell University Press, Ithaca, 1999)

Janssen, J., 'Absence from Work by the Necropolis Workmen of Thebes', *Studien zur Altagyptischen Kultur.* Band 8 pp.127-152 (1980)

Janssen, J., *Commodity Prices from the Ramesside Period* (E.J. Brill, Leiden, 1975)

Janssen, R., and Janssen, J., *Getting Old in Ancient Egypt* (Rubicon Press, London. 1996)

Janssen, R., and Janssen., J, *Growing Up in Ancient Egypt (*Rubicon Press, London, 1990)

Janssen, R., 'Costume in New Kingdom Egypt', in Sasson J.M., (Ed) *Civilizations of the Ancient Near East. Vol I* (Charles Scribners Sons, New York, 1995)

Kemp, B., *Ancient Egypt. Anatomy of a Civilisation* (Routledge, London, 1989)

Lehner, M., 'The Sphinx: Who built it, and why?', in *Archaeologist* (September/October 1994, pp32-41)

Lesko, L., *Pharaohs' Workers (*Cornell University Press, London, 1994)

Lichtheim, M., *Ancient Egyptian Literature. Vol. I. The Old and Middle Kingdom* (University of California Press, Berkeley, 1973)

Lichtheim, M., *Ancient Egyptian Literature. Vol. III. The Late Period* (University of California Press, Berkeley, 1980)

Lichtheim, M., *Ancient Egyptian Literature; Volume II. The New Kingdom (*University of California Press, Berkeley, 1976)

Lurker, M., *The Gods and Symbols of Ancient Egypt* (Thames and Hudson, London, 1974)

Manniche, L., *An Ancient Egyptian Herbal* (British Museum Press, London, 1989)

Manniche, L., *Sacred Luxuries: Fragrance, Aromatherapy and Cosmetics in Ancient Egypt* (Opus Publishers Ltd, London, 1999)

Manniche, L., *Sexual Life in Ancient Egypt* (Kegan Paul Press, London, 1997)

McDowell, A.G. *Village Life in Ancient Egypt: Laundry Lists and Love Songs.* (Oxford University Press, Oxford, 1991)

Nunn, J., *Ancient Egyptian Medicine* (British Museum Press, London, 1996)

Parkinson, R., *Voices from Ancient Egypt (*British Museum Press, London, 1991)

Quirke, S., *Ancient Egyptian Religion (*British Museum Press, London, 1992)

Quirke, S., *Lahun: a town in Egypt 1800BC, and the history and its landscape (*Golden House Publications, London, 2005)

Reeves, C., *Egyptian Medicine* (Shire Egyptology, Stroud, 1992)

Robins, G., *Women in Ancient Egypt* (British Museum Press, London, 1993)

Save Soderbergh, T., *Pharaohs and Mortals* (Robert Hale Limited, London, 1958)

Shaw, I., and Nicholson, P., *British Museum Dictionary of Ancient Egypt* (British Museum Press, London, 1995)

Spencer, A.J., *Death in Ancient Egypt* (Penguin, London, 1991)

Stetter, C., *The Secret Medicine of the Pharaohs; Ancient Egyptian Healing* (Edition Q, Chicago, 1993)

Strouhal, E., *Life in Ancient Egypt* (Liverpool University Press, Liverpool, 1992)

Taterka, F., 'The Black Eye-Paint of Punt', in *Luxor Times Magazine*, Issue 1. (2008)

Taylor, J., *Death and the Afterlife in Ancient Egypt* (British Museum Press, London, 2001)

Tydesley, J., *Hatshepsut; the Female Pharaoh* (Viking, London, 1996)

Tydesley, J., *The Daughters of Isis* (Viking, London, 1994)

Tyldesley, J., *Judgement of Pharaoh* (Phoenix, London, 2000)

Tyldesley, J.. *Egyptian Games and Sports* (Shire, Stroud, 2007)

Uphill, E., *Egyptian Towns and Cities* (Shire, Stroud, 2001)

Vogelsang-Eastwood, G.M., *Tutankhamun's Wardrobe* (Barjesteh van Waalwijk van Doorn & Co, Rotterdam, 1999)

Watterson, B., *Women in Ancient Egypt* (Sutton Publishing, Gloucestershire, 1991)

White, J.M., *Everyday Life in Ancient Egypt* (B.T. Batsford. London, 1963)

Wilkinson, R.H., *The Complete Gods and Goddesses of Ancient Egypt.* (Thames and Hudson, London, 2003)

Index